AFOQT

Study Guide

2024/2025

Exam Prep Book for the Air Force Officer Qualifying Test:

700+ Practice Questions and detailed answers.

By

Jeff Hosmer

CHAPTER 1: INTRODUCTION

Welcome, future Air Force officer! If you've picked up this book, you're likely on the path to taking one of the most important exams of your military career—the Air Force Officer Qualifying Test, or AFOQT for short. This isn't just another test; it's a defining moment that can shape your future in the United States Air Force.

The Significance of the AFOQT

So, why is the AFOQT so important? Well, it's not merely a formality. This comprehensive test assesses a wide range of skills and aptitudes, from your verbal and mathematical abilities to your spatial awareness and situational judgment. The Air Force uses your scores to determine if you've got what it takes to be an officer. Excelling in this test can open up a world of opportunities, from pilot training to specialized roles in areas like intelligence and logistics.

The Role of the AFOQT in Career Eligibility

Your performance on the AFOQT doesn't just give you bragging rights; it plays a crucial role in determining your eligibility for different career paths within the Air Force. Alongside other factors like your educational background and physical fitness, your AFOQT scores can make you a more appealing candidate for competitive roles. Conversely, lower scores might limit your options. So, think of the AFOQT not as a hurdle but as an opportunity to shine.

The Impact on Your Military Journey

Taking the AFOQT is a significant step in your military journey. Your scores will not only influence the career paths available to you but also affect future training opportunities and even the timing of your promotions. In essence, this test is more than a one-day event; it's a milestone that can shape your entire career in the Air Force.

What to Expect from This Book

You're probably wondering what this book has to offer. Well, we've got you covered. The book is structured into 12 core sections, each focusing on one of the AFOQT's subtests. In each section, you'll find a concise review of essential concepts, followed by practice questions to test your understanding, and sharpen your skills.

And here's the cherry on top: we've included insider tips and tricks from experienced Air Force officers. These golden nuggets of wisdom will give you a unique perspective on tackling questions and managing your time during the exam.

Bonus: Flash Card App

As a special bonus, this book comes with access to a flash card app designed to reinforce key concepts and improve your recall speed. It's a handy tool that you can use anytime, anywhere to make your study sessions more effective.

Wrapping It Up

The book rounds off with two full-length practice tests, featuring over 1200 questions along with detailed answers and explanations. These tests are designed to simulate the real AFOQT experience, helping you gauge your readiness, identify areas for improvement, and boost your confidence.

Whether you're a seasoned test-taker or a newcomer to the AFOQT, this guide aims to provide you with all the tools you'll need to ace the test and pave the way for a fulfilling career in the U.S. Air Force. So, let's turn the page and dive into the first subtest: Verbal Analogies. Your journey to becoming an Air Force officer starts now.

CHAPTER 2: VERBAL ANALOGIES

Welcome to the Verbal Analogies chapter! If you've ever played word association games or enjoyed figuring out how words relate to each other, then you're already familiar with the essence of this subtest. Verbal Analogies assess your ability to see relationships between words, and it's a crucial part of the AFOQT. So, let's dive in and get you prepared.

Understanding Word Relationships

Ah, the fascinating world of word relationships! If you've ever marveled at how words can be intricately connected, then you're in for a treat. Understanding these connections is the cornerstone of the Verbal Analogies subtest.

Synonyms: The Like-Minded Pals

Think of synonyms as best friends who almost always agree with each other. Words like "happy" and "joyful" or "quick" and "fast" are synonyms because they share similar meanings. When you see a pair of words that seem to be nodding in agreement, you're likely looking at synonyms.

Antonyms: The Friendly Rivals

Antonyms are like siblings who love each other but have opposite tastes. Words like "hot" and "cold" or "up" and "down" are classic examples. They represent opposite ends of the spectrum but are related in that they define each other by their differences.

Parts to Whole: The Team Players

In this relationship, one word is a part of the other, much like a wheel is a part of a car. It's like how a goalie is crucial to a soccer team but is just one part of the whole squad. Recognizing these relationships requires you to think about how smaller elements contribute to larger entities.

Cause and Effect: The Action and Reaction

Some words are connected through a cause-and-effect relationship. For example, "rain" and "flood" or "study" and "learn." In these pairs, the first word triggers the second. It's like planting a seed and watching a flower bloom; one action leads to a result.

Abstract Relationships: The Thinkers

Sometimes, the relationship between words isn't straightforward. It could be thematic, like "pen" and "write," where one word describes the function of the other. Or it could be sequential, like "baby" and "toddler," indicating stages of development. These require a bit more thought but are incredibly satisfying to figure out.

The Speed Factor

Time is of the essence in the AFOQT. Recognizing these relationships quickly can give you a significant edge. The faster you identify the relationship between the words in the question, the quicker you can spot the same relationship among the answer choices.

The Accuracy Element

Speed is crucial, but accuracy is king. It's not just about how fast you can answer the questions, but how accurately you can do so. The more you practice, the better you'll get at quickly identifying the correct relationships without second-guessing yourself.

So, as you go through your practice questions, keep these types of relationships in mind. The more familiar you become with them, the more confident you'll feel on test day. And remember, you've got this!

Building Your Vocabulary

Ah, vocabulary—the unsung hero of any language-based test. When it comes to verbal analogies, having a robust vocabulary isn't just a nice-to-have; it's essential. Think of it as your toolkit. The more tools you have, the better equipped you'll be to tackle any challenge that comes your way.

The Power of Words

Words are more than just a collection of letters; they're the building blocks of understanding. Knowing a word isn't just about knowing its definition. It's about understanding its nuances, its connotations, and the context in which it's used. This deeper understanding will enable you to identify relationships quickly and accurately between words, which is the crux of the Verbal Analogies subtest.

Don't Skip, Dig Deeper

Let's be real; it's tempting to skip over words you don't know. But every word you skip is a missed opportunity for growth. So, the next time you stumble upon an unfamiliar word, pause, and look it up. Dive into its meaning, its synonyms, and even its antonyms. Try to use it in a sentence or two. This active engagement will help cement the word in your memory.

The Ripple Effect

And here's the best part: improving your vocabulary doesn't just help you in this subtest; it has a ripple effect that benefits you in other areas too. A strong vocabulary can improve your communication skills, enhance your ability to express yourself, and even boost your confidence. It's like a Swiss Army knife that comes in handy in various situations, both in tests and in life.

Make It a Habit

Incorporate vocabulary building into your daily routine. Whether it's learning a new word each day, reading articles that challenge you, or even engaging in conversations that push you out of your comfort zone, every little bit helps. And hey, there's an app for that! Many vocabulary-building apps can make this process interactive and fun.

Pro Tip: Flashcards Are Your Friend

Remember the flash card app that comes as a bonus with this book It's a goldmine for vocabulary building. Use it to create flashcards for new words you encounter. Review them regularly and test yourself to see how many you remember. It's a simple yet effective way to reinforce what you've learned.

Practice Makes Perfect

Alright, let's roll up our sleeves and get into the nitty-gritty—practice questions. You know, there's something genuinely satisfying about tackling these questions head-on. It's like a mental gym session, and each question is a weight you're lifting to build your mental muscles. So, let's get to it!

First off, don't sweat it if you get some questions wrong. Seriously, it's okay. Mistakes are like little signposts on your learning journey, pointing out where you need to focus your energy. The key is not to breeze past them but to pause and reflect. Ask yourself, "Why did I choose that answer? What was my thought process?" This self-reflection is invaluable; it's how you turn a simple mistake into a learning opportunity.

And hey, don't be too hard on yourself. This is a practice session, not the actual exam. The whole point is to identify your strengths and weaknesses, so you know exactly where to focus your study time. Think of each question as a mini lesson in verbal reasoning. Whether you get it right or wrong, there's something valuable to be learned.

Remember, practice isn't just about repetition; it's about mindful repetition. It's the difference between mindlessly running laps and training for a marathon with a well-thought-out regimen. So, as you go through these practice questions, be present. Take your time to read each question carefully, consider your options, and make your best guess. Then, regardless of whether you got it right or wrong, read the explanation. Understand the 'why' behind the answer, and you'll be better prepared for similar questions in the future.

So, are you ready to flex those mental muscles and dive into some practice questions? Let's do this! And remember, you're not just practicing for a test; you're practicing for your future in the U.S. Air Force. How's that for motivation?

Sample Practice Questions

Alright, let's dig a little deeper into these sample questions. I know, practice questions might not be everyone's idea of a good time, but they're the bread and butter of test prep. Plus, understanding the 'why' behind the answer can be incredibly satisfying. So, let's get into it.

Apple: Fruit :: Oak : ?

Choices:

A) Tree

B) Leaf

C) Wood

D) Forest

Expanded Explanation:

Think of it this way: an apple is a specific example of a fruit, right? In the same vein, an oak is a specific example of what? A tree, of course! So, the relationship here is "specific to general," or you could say "part to whole." An apple falls under the category of fruit, and an oak falls under the category of trees. The correct answer is A) Tree.

Write : Pen :: Cut : ?

Choices:

A) Knife

B) Scissors

C) Paper

D) Board

Expanded Explanation:

Imagine you're writing a letter. What do you need? A pen. Now, picture yourself wrapping a gift. You'll need something to cut the wrapping paper. It could be a knife or scissors. So, the relationship is "tool to action." You use a pen to write and a knife or scissors to cut. This means both A) Knife and B) Scissors are correct. Tricky, huh?

Happy : Joyful :: Sad : ?

Choices:

A) Angry

B) Tearful

C) Mournful

D) Excited

Expanded Explanation:

This one's all about emotions and synonyms. If you're happy, another word to describe that feeling could be joyful. Now, if you're sad, another word that captures that emotion is mournful. So, the relationship here is based on synonyms. Happy is another way to say joyful, and sad is another way to say mournful. The correct answer is C) Mournful.

Pro Tip: Eliminate and Conquer - A Closer Look

Let's talk strategy for a moment. The "eliminate and conquer" method is like your secret weapon for tackling tricky questions. Say you're stumped and can't decide between two or more options. Start by crossing out the answers that just don't fit. For example, in the "Write : Pen :: Cut : ?" question, you could easily eliminate C) Paper and D) Board because you don't use paper or a board to cut something. Now you're left with just two options, increasing your chances of getting it right. It's a simple but effective way to improve your odds.

So, there you have it! A deeper dive into some sample questions and a pro tip to boot. Keep these strategies in mind as you tackle more practice questions, and you'll be well on your way to mastering verbal analogies.

CHAPTER 3: ARITHMETIC REASONING

Welcome to the Arithmetic Reasoning chapter! You might be wondering, "Why do I need to know about fractions and percentages for a military test?" Well, arithmetic reasoning is more than just numbers; it's about problem-solving and logical thinking—skills you'll need in the Air Force. So, let's get you comfortable with these concepts.

Fractions: The Building Blocks - A Deeper Dive

Ah, fractions! They're like the unsung heroes of the math world. You might not give them much thought, but they're working behind the scenes in so many aspects of life. Remember sharing a pizza with friends? Each slice is a fraction of the whole pizza. Or think about when you're checking your car's fuel efficiency; you're dealing with miles per gallon, another fraction.

What's in a Fraction?

Let's break it down. A fraction has two parts: the numerator and the denominator. The numerator, the top number, tells you how many parts you have. The denominator, the bottom number, tells you how many parts make up a whole. So, if you have a fraction like $\frac{3}{4}$, it means you have 3 parts out of a whole divided into 4 equal parts.

Real-World Applications

You might be wondering, "Why should I care?" Well, fractions are more than just numbers on paper; they're practical tools. For instance, if you're into cooking, you'll often find recipes that require $\frac{1}{2}$ a cup of sugar or $\frac{3}{4}$ teaspoon of salt. Or maybe you're into sports analytics, where player statistics are often represented as fractions.

Fractions in the Air Force

In a military setting, fractions can be crucial. Imagine you're an Air Force pilot, and you need to distribute fuel equally among multiple aircraft. You'll need a solid understanding of fractions to get it right. Or perhaps you're in logistics, calculating the distribution of supplies. Again, fractions to the rescue!

Percentages: More Than Just Grades

Ah, percentages. You've probably encountered them in school when eagerly (or nervously) awaiting your test scores. But let's be real, percentages are everywhere, not just in the classroom. Whether you're tipping at a restaurant, calculating the interest on a loan, or even figuring out how much of your paycheck goes to taxes, percentages are a part of daily life.

The Basics: What's in a Percentage?

So, what exactly is a percentage? In essence, it's a fraction with a denominator of 100. When you see "50%," think $\frac{50}{100}$, which simplifies to $\frac{1}{2}$ or 0.5. It's a way to express a part of a whole, just like fractions, but it's often easier to visualize. If someone says, "You got 90% on your test," you instantly know you did well. If they said, "You got $\frac{18}{20}$," it might take you a moment to realize that's also 90%.

REAL-WORLD APPLICATIONS

Let's get practical for a moment. Imagine you're at a store, and you see a sign that says "25% off." What does that mean for you? It means you're about to save some money! To find out how much, you'd take the original price and multiply it by 0.25 (the decimal form of 25%). That gives you the discount amount, which you then subtract from the original price. Voila! You've just used percentages in real life.

Converting Fractions to Percentages: It's Easier Than You Think

Now, how do you go from a fraction to a percentage? It's a piece of cake. Divide the numerator by the denominator, and then multiply the result by 100. For example, to convert $\frac{3}{4}$ x 100= 75. See? You're already becoming a percentages pro.

Pro Tip: The Reverse is Also True

Here's a quick tip: you can also convert percentages back to fractions or decimals. To convert 75% back to a fraction, you'd divide 75 by 100 to get $\frac{3}{4}$ .It's like having a mathematical Swiss Army knife in your pocket.

So, the next time you see a percentage, whether it's on a test, a sale sign, or even a nutrition label, you'll know exactly what it means and how to work with it. And that, my friend, is the power of understanding percentages.

Ratios: The Art of Comparison

Ah, ratios. They're like the unsung heroes of arithmetic reasoning. You might not think about them often, but when you do need them, they're invaluable. Whether you're trying to figure out the right fuel-to-oil mix for an aircraft or planning how many troops are needed for different tasks, ratios are your go-to tool. So, let's get cozy with them, shall we?

The Basics Revisited

A ratio is essentially a relationship between two numbers, indicating how many times one value is contained within the other. For instance, if you have a bag of 5 red balls and 3 blue balls, the ratio of red to blue balls is 5 to 3. You can express this relationship in three ways: as a fraction $\frac{5}{3}$, with a colon 5:3, or in words "5 to 3."

Real-World Applications

Imagine you're an Air Force pilot, and you need to mix fuel and oil in a specific ratio for optimal engine performance. If the ratio is off, you could be looking at engine failure, and nobody wants that. Or picture yourself in a strategic planning meeting where you have to allocate resources—like personnel and equipment—based on specific ratios to achieve mission objectives. Understanding ratios can literally be a lifesaver.

Ratios in Everyday Life

But ratios aren't just for high-stakes military scenarios. Think about cooking. Ever tried to scale a recipe up or down? You're using ratios. Or what about mixing paint colors? Yep, ratios again. They're everywhere, and the better you understand them, the easier a lot of everyday tasks become.

Practice Makes Perfect

Let's put your newfound knowledge to the test with a couple of practice questions:

1. If you have a bag containing 4 red balls, 3 blue balls, and 5 green balls, what is the ratio of red to blue to green balls?
2. You need to mix a cleaning solution with water in a 3:7 ratio. How much cleaning solution will you need if you have 28 ounces of water?

Tips and Tricks

Here's a pro tip: when dealing with ratios, always simplify them to their lowest terms, just like you would with fractions. It makes calculations easier and less prone to error. And remember, ratios are all about comparison, so keep an eye on what you're comparing to what.

Ratios might seem simple, but they're incredibly versatile and useful, both in high-stakes situations and in everyday life. Keep practicing, and you'll become a ratio pro in no time.

Decimals and Square Roots

Just when you thought we were done, we're diving into decimals and square roots. These might seem intimidating, but they're just another way to express numbers. Decimals are fractions in disguise, and square roots are all about finding that number which, when multiplied by itself, gives you the original number. Simple, right?

Decimals: Fractions in Disguise

Decimals are fractions that have been converted to base 10. For example, $\frac{1}{2}$ is the same as 0.5. Understanding decimals is crucial for tasks like calculating distances or speeds. To convert a fraction to a decimal, you divide the numerator by the denominator.

Square Roots: The Hidden Gem

Square roots might seem complex, but they're just numbers waiting to be multiplied by themselves. For example, the square root of 25 is 5 because 5×5=25. Square roots are particularly useful in fields like engineering and navigation.

More Practice Questions: Challenge Yourself

Feeling confident? Let's ramp up the difficulty with some more practice questions. Remember, the aim is to understand the concept, not just to find the right answer.

1. Convert 0.75 to a fraction.
2. What is the square root of 64?
3. If a rectangle has a length of 8 and a width of 6, what is the ratio of length to width?

DETAILED EXPLANATIONS: - THE ANSWERS UNVEILED

Explanation for Convert 0.75 to a Fraction

The decimal 0.75 can be converted to $\frac{75}{100}$, and when simplified, it becomes $\frac{3}{4}$. Converting decimals to fractions is like translating one language to another; the meaning stays the same, just the expression changes.

Explanation for What is the Square Root of 64?

The square root of 64 is 8 because 8×8=64. Square roots can seem elusive, but once you get the hang of them, they're just another way to express a number's relationship with itself.

Explanation for Rectangle Ratio

The rectangle has a length of 8 and a width of 6, so the ratio of length to width is 8:6. When simplified, this becomes 4:3. Ratios are all about relationships, and in this case, it's about how the length relates to the width.

Sample Practice Questions

Alright, you've been absorbing all this information, and now it's time to put it to work. Think of this as the gym session after the theory class. You've got the knowledge; now let's build those mental muscles. And hey, if you stumble a bit, that's perfectly okay. Mistakes are just stepping stones on the path to mastery. So, let's dive in!

Question 1: Fractions in Action

You have a pie divided into 8 slices. You and your friend eat 3 slices. What fraction of the pie is left?

Question 2: Percentages in Real Life

Your favorite store is offering a 20% discount on a jacket that originally costs $100. How much will the jacket cost after the discount?

Question 3: Ratio Rundown

You're mixing a protein shake that calls for a 2:1 ratio of milk to protein powder. If you use 16 ounces of milk, how much protein powder will you need?

Question 4: Decimal Dilemma

Convert $\frac{3}{4}$ to a decimal.

Question 5: Square Root Challenge

What is the square root of 121?

Question 6: Bonus Question - Mix It Up

You have a bag of 6 red balls, 4 blue balls, and 5 green balls. What is the ratio of red to blue to green balls?

Take a Breather and Reflect

Once you've given these questions your best shot, take a moment to breathe. Seriously, take a deep breath. How did it feel? Were there moments of "Aha!" or perhaps some "Oh no, why did I do that?" Either way, it's all part of the learning process.

Up Next: Detailed Explanations

Don't rush off to check your answers just yet. Take a minute to think about how you approached each question. Did you use any of the tips or tricks we discussed? Once you've done that mental recap, head over to the 'Detailed Explanations' section. There, you'll find not just the answers, but the 'why' behind them. It's like having a cozy chat with a mentor who guides you through the tricky spots.

So, are you ready to see how you did? Let's move on and uncover the magic behind the right answers. And remember, whether you nailed all the questions or are still finding your footing, you're making progress, and that's what counts.

DETAILED EXPLANATIONS

So, you've tackled the practice questions, and hopefully, you're buzzing with that "I did it!" energy. But whether you aced them or found a few stumbling blocks, this is where the real learning kicks in. Let's break down each question and see what makes the right answer tick.

Explanation for Question 1: Fractions in Action

You started with 8 slices of pie and ate 3, leaving you with 5 slices. The fraction of the pie left is $\frac{5}{8}$. See? Fractions are just a way to express parts of a whole, and in this case, the 'whole' is your delicious pie.

Explanation for Question 2: Percentages in Real Life

A 20% discount on a $100 jacket means you save $20. So, the jacket will now cost you $80. Percentages are just fractions or ratios expressed in terms of 100, and they pop up all the time in real life, especially when shopping.

Explanation for Question 3: Ratio Rundown

The ratio is 2:1 of milk to protein powder. You used 16 ounces of milk, so you'll need half that amount in protein powder, which is 8 ounces. Ratios help you keep proportions consistent, whether you're making a protein shake or mixing fuel for a jet.

Explanation for Question 4: Decimal Dilemma

The fraction $\frac{3}{4}$ converts to the decimal 0.75 when you divide 3 by 4. Decimals and fractions are two sides of the same coin and knowing how to switch between them is a useful skill.

Explanation for Question 5: Square Root Challenge

The square root of 121 is 11 because 11×11=121. Square roots might seem intimidating, but they're just about finding that special number that, when multiplied by itself, gives you back your original number.

Explanation for Question 6: Bonus Question - Mix It Up

You have 6 red balls, 4 blue balls, and 5 green balls. The ratio is 6:4:5. Remember, ratios are all about comparing different quantities to each other, and in this case, you're comparing the counts of different colored balls.

Final Nuggets of Wisdom

So, there you have it—the detailed breakdown of each practice question. Whether you breezed through them or had a couple of "Oops!" moments, I hope you gained some insights into the 'why' behind the 'what.' Keep these explanations in mind as you tackle more questions, and you'll find that the concepts start to click into place like pieces of a puzzle.

And hey, don't forget to use that bonus flash card app that comes with this book. It's a fantastic tool for quick reviews and on-the-go learning. Keep practicing, stay curious, and you'll be well on your way to acing the AFOQT.

CHAPTER 4: WORD KNOWLEDGE

Welcome to the Word Knowledge subtest chapter! Words are the building blocks of communication, and a strong vocabulary is like having a Swiss Army knife in your mental toolkit. Whether you're reading technical manuals or issuing commands, the words you choose can make a world of difference. So, let's dive in and sharpen that verbal edge of yours.

Understanding Word Meanings

Words often have multiple meanings depending on the context in which they're used. Take the word "lead," for example. It could mean to guide someone, or it could refer to the metal. Understanding the context is crucial for pinpointing the word's intended meaning. A good strategy is to read the entire sentence or even the surrounding sentences to get a clear picture.

Synonyms: The Spice of Language

Synonyms are words that have similar meanings, like 'happy' and 'joyful.' Knowing synonyms can be a real asset, especially when you're trying to avoid repetition or find the most fitting word for a situation. A handy tip is to group synonyms together in your mind. Think of them as a family where everyone shares a common trait but has their unique quirks.

Antonyms: The Flip Side

Antonyms are the opposites of synonyms, literally. They're words with opposite meanings, like 'hot' and 'cold.' Knowing antonyms is just as important as knowing synonyms. They help you understand contrasts and make your communication more dynamic. A useful trick is to add the prefix 'un-' or 'dis-' to a word in your mind and see if it creates a valid antonym. For example, 'happy' becomes 'unhappy.'

Practice Questions: Your Turn

Let's get those mental gears turning. Here are some practice questions to help you flex those vocabulary muscles.

What is the synonym of 'arduous'?

A) Easy

B) Difficult

C) Happy

D) Fast

What is the antonym of 'generous'?

A) Stingy

B) Kind

C) Large

D) Small

In the sentence "The project was a monumental failure," what does 'monumental' mean?

A) Small

B) Huge

C) Successful

D) Quick

Answers and Explanations

B) Difficult - 'Arduous' means requiring a lot of effort, which is similar to 'difficult.'

A) Stingy - The opposite of being generous is being stingy or not willing to give.

B) Huge - In this context, 'monumental' means significant or huge, emphasizing the scale of the failure.

CHAPTER 5: MATH KNOWLEDGE

Welcome to the chapter on Math Knowledge, a cornerstone of the AFOQT and a skill set that's indispensable in the Air Force. Whether you're calculating fuel ratios for a jet or figuring out the angles for a landing approach, math is more than numbers on a paper; it's a language of logic and precision. So, let's get started.

Algebra: The Foundation

Ah, algebra, the cornerstone of many mathematical problems you'll encounter, not just in tests but in real-world applications too. Think of algebra as the Swiss Army knife in your mathematical toolkit. It's versatile and essential, whether you're solving for fuel efficiency or planning complex operations. Let's break it down a bit.

Variables: The Unknowns

Variables are the mysterious elements in algebra. They stand in for unknown quantities, waiting to be revealed. In the Air Force, you'll often deal with unknowns—weather conditions, enemy positions, or fuel consumption rates. Learning to solve for variables in equations prepares you for solving real-world unknowns.

Equations: The Balancing Act

Equations are all about balance. On either side of that equal sign, things have to, well, equal out. It's like balancing the wings of an aircraft; everything needs to be in harmony for the equation to "fly." You'll often find yourself setting up equations to solve problems, from calculating airspeed to determining payload capacity.

Expressions: The Building Blocks

Expressions are the phrases of the algebraic language. They can be as simple as 'x + 2' or as complex as '$2x^2 + 3xy - 4y^2$.' Understanding expressions is like understanding the components of an aircraft; each part has its role and knowing how they fit together helps you see the bigger picture.

The Order of Operations: PEMDAS

Remember the acronym PEMDAS? Parentheses, Exponents, Multiplication and Division (from left to right), Addition and Subtraction (from left to right). This is your roadmap for tackling any algebraic expression. It's like the checklist pilots go through before takeoff; it ensures you solve equations in the right order.

Practice Makes Perfect

The key to mastering algebra is practice. The more you work with variables, equations, and expressions, the more intuitive they become. It's like flight hours; the more you have, the better pilot you become.

Sample Questions

- Solve for x: $3x+4=13$
- Simplify the expression: $2x-3+4x+5$
- Solve the equation for y: $2y-3=5+y$

Answers and Explanations

1. x=3 - To solve for x, first subtract 4 from both sides to get 3x=9. Then divide both sides by 3.
2. 6x+2 - Combine like terms to simplify the expression.
3. y=8 - First, subtract y from both sides to get y=8. Then solve for y.

So, there you have it, a quick but comprehensive dive into the world of algebra. It's not just numbers and letters on a page; it's a skill set that will serve you well in any Air Force role. Keep practicing, and you'll find that these 'unknowns' become known quantities in no time.

Geometry: Shapes and Spaces

Ah, geometry, the study of shapes and spaces. It's like the architecture of the mathematical world, and in the Air Force, it's the blueprint for understanding the world around you. Whether you're trying to figure out the best angle for a landing approach or calculating the area needed for a temporary airstrip, geometry is your go-to tool. Let's break it down a bit more.

Lines and Angles

Lines and angles are the ABCs of geometry. You've got your straight lines, your intersecting lines, and don't forget those parallel lines that never meet—kind of like two planes flying in formation but never crossing paths. Angles come in various flavors too: acute, obtuse, and right angles. Knowing how to identify and work with these basics is like learning the chords on a guitar; it sets the foundation for everything else.

Polygons: More than Just Shapes

Polygons are like the building blocks of geometric structures. Triangles, rectangles, and hexagons are all polygons. In the Air Force, think of polygons as the shapes that make up everything from the design of an aircraft wing to the layout of a base. Understanding the properties of these shapes can help you make quick and accurate calculations. For example, knowing that the interior angles of a triangle always sum up to 180 degrees can be a real time-saver.

Circles: The Loop of Geometry

Circles are everywhere in aviation: from the shape of a jet engine to the radar screens. The key terms here are radius, diameter, and circumference. A circle is a beautiful thing in geometry because it's so constant; the ratio of its circumference to its diameter is always π (Pi), a mathematical constant. Circles are smooth, predictable, and in aviation, that's often exactly what you need.

3D Geometry: Adding Another Layer

Let's not forget about the third dimension. In 3D geometry, you're dealing with shapes like spheres, cylinders, and pyramids. This is the geometry of air traffic control, of understanding how aircraft occupy space, not just on a flat map but in the sky, ascending and descending.

Trigonometry: Angles and Ratios

Ah, trigonometry—the branch of math that has a way of making people's eyes glaze over. But let's demystify it, shall we? Trigonometry is far from abstract; it's incredibly practical, especially in aviation. Imagine you're piloting an aircraft. The angles and ratios you calculate could be the difference between a smooth landing and—well, let's not go there.

Understanding the Basics

Trigonometry is fundamentally about triangles, specifically right-angled triangles. The three main trigonometric functions you'll encounter are sine (sin), cosine (cos), and tangent (tan). These functions help you relate the angles of a triangle to the lengths of its sides.

SOH-CAH-TOA: Your New Best Friend

Remember this mnemonic: SOH-CAH-TOA. It stands for Sine equals Opposite over Hypotenuse, Cosine equals Adjacent over Hypotenuse, and Tangent equals Opposite over Adjacent. This little phrase is like a pocket guide to trigonometry. Keep it in your mental back pocket; it'll come in handy more often than you think.

Real-World Applications

In the Air Force, trigonometry is everywhere. It's in the navigation systems, in the angles of radar, and even in the calculations for fuel efficiency during long-haul flights. Understanding trigonometry can give you a real edge, whether you're in the cockpit, the control room, or on the engineering team.

Practice Makes Perfect

Let's get some skin in the game. How about a couple of practice questions to solidify these concepts?

1. Calculate the cosine of a 60-degree angle.
2. If the opposite side is 4 and the adjacent side is 3 in a right-angled triangle, what is the tangent?

Pro Tip: Unit Circle Magic

The unit circle is a fantastic tool for understanding trigonometric functions. It's a circle with a radius of one, centered at the origin of a Cartesian coordinate system. As you move around the circle, the sine and cosine values correspond to the y and x coordinates, respectively. It's like having a trigonometric cheat sheet right in front of you.

So, there you have it—trigonometry in a nutshell. It's not just about solving problems on paper; it's a skill that has real, tangible applications in your Air Force career. So, embrace those triangles and ratios; they're more than just shapes and numbers— they're the building blocks of logical reasoning and problem-solving.

Answers and Explanations

Cosine of 60 degrees is 0.5.

Tangent is Opposite/Adjacent, so 4/3, which is approximately 1.33.

Practice Questions: Let's Get to Work

Alright, you've made it this far, and that's something to be proud of. Now, let's put that newfound knowledge to the test with some practice questions. Remember, it's not just about getting the right answer; it's about understanding how you got there. So, take a deep breath, grab that pencil, and let's dive in.

Algebra

1. Solve for x in the equation 3x+4=13.
2. If 2y−7=9, what is y?

Geometry

1. What is the area of a rectangle with a length of 10 units and a width of 5 units?
2. A triangle has one angle measuring 90 degrees and another measuring 45 degrees. What is the measure of the third angle?

Trigonometry

1. Calculate the cosine of a 60-degree angle.
2. If the opposite side of a right triangle is 4 and the adjacent side is 3, what is the tangent of the angle?

Don't rush through these. Take your time, and if you find yourself stuck, it's okay to take a step back and revisit the concepts. The beauty of math is that it's not a sprint; it's a marathon. And every question you tackle is another stride toward your goal.

ANSWERS AND EXPLANATIONS

Algebra Question 1:

To solve 3x+4=13, you'll first want to isolate x on one side of the equation. Subtract 4 from both sides to get 3x=9. Then, divide both sides by 3 to find x=3.

Algebra Question 2:

For 2y−7=9, add 7 to both sides to get 2y=16. Divide both sides by 2, and you'll find y=8.

Geometry Question 1:

The area of a rectangle is found by multiplying the length and the width. So, 10×5=50 square units.

Geometry Question 2:

In a triangle, the sum of all angles is 180 degrees. You already have one angle of 90 degrees and another of 45 degrees. Add those together to get 135 degrees. Subtract that from 180, and the third angle is 45 degrees.

Trigonometry Question 1:

The cosine of a 60-degree angle is 0.5.

Trigonometry Question 2:

The tangent of an angle in a right triangle is the opposite side divided by the adjacent side. So, $\frac{4}{3} \approx 1.333$.

CHAPTER 6: INSTRUMENT COMPREHENSION

If you're aiming for a role in aviation, this section is your bread and butter. Even if you're not, understanding these instruments can give you a leg up in various Air Force positions. Let's dive into the basics of reading and interpreting aviation instruments, shall we?

The Altimeter: Your Vertical GPS

Ah, the altimeter, a pilot's best friend when it comes to understanding how high you're flying. Imagine you're cruising in the sky, and you see a mountain range ahead. Your altimeter is what tells you whether you're flying high enough to pass over those peaks or if you need to climb a bit more to avoid becoming an unwanted part of the landscape.

How It Works

The altimeter operates on air pressure. As you ascend, the air pressure decreases, and the altimeter's hands move to indicate your new altitude. It's like a barometer but calibrated specifically for aviation. So, when you look at it, you're not just seeing numbers; you're getting real-time feedback from the atmosphere itself.

The Three-Pointer System

Most altimeters have a three-pointer system. The shortest hand shows tens of thousands of feet, the middle one indicates thousands, and the longest hand represents hundreds. It's like reading a clock, but instead of telling time, you're measuring your distance from sea level.

When to Check It

You'll want to glance at your altimeter frequently, especially during crucial phases of flight like takeoff, landing, and when navigating through tricky terrain. It's not just a "set it and forget it" instrument; it's a dynamic tool that needs your attention.

Real-World Applications

Beyond avoiding mountains, the altimeter is vital for other aspects of flying. For instance, air traffic control might assign you a specific altitude to maintain during your flight. Or perhaps you're in a holding pattern, waiting for clearance to land; your altimeter ensures you stay at the correct height while circling.

A Word of Caution

While the altimeter is incredibly useful, it's not infallible. Factors like drastic changes in weather can affect its accuracy. That's why it's essential to cross-reference it with other instruments and navigational aids. Trust but verify, as they say.

The Airspeed Indicator: Your In-Flight Speedometer

Ah, the airspeed indicator, a pilot's best friend when it comes to speed. Imagine you're cruising down a highway; you'd glance at your car's speedometer now and then, right?

In the sky, the airspeed indicator serves a similar purpose but with even higher stakes. Let's get cozy with this essential instrument.

How It Works

The airspeed indicator is a dynamic piece of equipment. It uses air pressure differences to calculate your speed. When you're up there, soaring through the clouds, it's not just the wind against your face; it's also the data feeding into this nifty gauge.

The Color-Coded Zones

Ever notice the color bands on the dial? They're not for decoration; each color serves a purpose. The green zone is your safe operating speed, the yellow is cautionary, and the red—well, let's just say you don't want to be in the red. It's the "pull up, pull up!" of aviation.

True Airspeed vs. Indicated Airspeed

Here's a tidbit that might surprise you: the airspeed indicator doesn't show your actual speed over the ground. That's your 'true airspeed,' and it's affected by wind and other factors. What you're seeing is the 'indicated airspeed,' which is your speed relative to the air around you. It's like the difference between how fast you're swimming in a river and how fast you're actually moving if the river is flowing.

Why It's Crucial

Let's get real for a second. Misreading your airspeed can lead to some dire situations. Too slow, and you risk a stall, which is like the airplane version of your car stalling but way scarier. Too fast, and you're looking at structural damage or, worse, losing control of the aircraft. This isn't a game; it's about making sure you and everyone on board stay safe.

Quick Tips

1. Always Cross-Check: Don't rely solely on the airspeed indicator. Cross-reference it with other instruments for a fuller picture of your flight status.
2. Mind the Conditions: Weather can affect your airspeed. Be extra vigilant during turbulent conditions.

3. Know Your Aircraft: Different planes have different optimal speeds. Make sure you're familiar with the aircraft you're piloting.

So, the next time you're up there, give a nod to your airspeed indicator. It's more than just numbers and needles; it's a guardian angel that helps you navigate the skies safely. Keep an eye on it, understand what it's telling you, and you'll be one step closer to acing that AFOQT and securing your dream role in the Air Force.

The Attitude Indicator: Your Skyward Compass

If only it could tell us if the plane is having a good or bad day, right? Jokes aside, this instrument is like your sixth sense in the sky. It's not just a gauge with some lines and colors; it's your immediate connection to the plane's orientation.

The Parts

The Attitude Indicator has two primary components: the miniature aircraft and the horizon bar. The miniature aircraft represents—you guessed it—your aircraft. The horizon bar separates the sky (usually blue) from the ground (usually brown or black). When the miniature aircraft is level with the horizon bar, you're flying straight and level.

Climbing and Descending

When the miniature aircraft is above the horizon bar, you're climbing. This is your visual cue that you're gaining altitude. Conversely, if the miniature aircraft is below the horizon bar, you're in a descent. It's as if the instrument is gently telling you, "Hey, we're going down; let's make sure that's intentional."

Turns and Tilts

The Attitude Indicator also shows if you're banking left or right. If the miniature aircraft tilts to one side, it's time to level your wings unless you're intentionally making a turn. Think of it as your plane giving you a nudge, saying, "Uh, you might want to check that."

Why It Matters

In the heat of a mission or during turbulent weather, the Attitude Indicator is your steadfast friend. It won't sugarcoat things or give you mixed signals. It tells you exactly what's happening with your plane, allowing you to make informed decisions quickly.

So, the next time you glance at the Attitude Indicator, know that it's more than just a piece of equipment. It's a vital part of your toolkit, a silent co-pilot that's always got your back. Keep an eye on it, understand what it's telling you, and you'll be a more competent, confident pilot. Now, how cool is that?

The Heading Indicator: Your Sky Compass

Think of it as your trusty compass, but instead of guiding you through a forest or across a desert, it's helping you navigate the vast expanse of the sky. It's a straightforward instrument, but don't let its simplicity fool you. Knowing how to read it correctly is crucial for everything from basic navigation to executing complex flight maneuvers.

Degrees and Directions

The Heading Indicator operates on a 360-degree scale, much like a traditional compass. Here's the kicker: North is represented as both 0 and 360 degrees. It's like coming full circle—literally. East is at 90 degrees, South sits at 180, and West rounds it out at 270 degrees.

Magnetic vs. True North

Here's a little nuance that can make a big difference: the Heading Indicator usually points to magnetic north, not true north. The difference between the two is called magnetic variation or declination, and it can vary depending on your geographical location. Always keep this in mind, especially when precise navigation is required.

Pre-flight Checks

Before taking off, it's a good habit to align your Heading Indicator with the magnetic compass. Why? Because the Heading Indicator can drift over time, and we don't want any surprises up there, do we?

In-Flight Adjustments

While you're up in the sky, it's not just "set it and forget it." Keep an eye on your Heading Indicator, especially during long flights. Periodic adjustments might be necessary to stay on course. A slight deviation might not seem like much, but over hundreds of miles, it can lead you way off target.

Quick Tips

1. Calibrate Before Flight: Always align with the magnetic compass.
2. Check Regularly: Make periodic checks to ensure you're on course.
3. Know Your Variation: Understand the magnetic variation for your flight area.

So, there you have it. The Heading Indicator might seem simple, but it's a cornerstone of safe and effective aviation. Whether you're flying cross-country or just around the block, this instrument is your steadfast guide through the skies.

Practice Questions: Time to Fly

Alright, let's put your newfound knowledge to the test with some practice questions.

What does the altimeter measure?

A) Speed

B) Direction

C) Altitude

D) Attitude

If the airspeed indicator shows 150 knots, what does that mean?

A) You're 150 miles from your destination.

B) You're flying at an altitude of 150 feet.

C) You're flying at 150 knots through the air.

D) You have 150 gallons of fuel left.

What does the attitude indicator show?

A) Your speed

B) Your altitude

C) Your aircraft's relation to the horizon

D) Your direction

If the heading indicator shows 90 degrees, which direction are you flying?

A) North

B) South

C) East

D) West

Answers and Explanations

Answer 1: C) Altitude

The altimeter measures your altitude or height above sea level.

Answer 2: C) You're flying at 150 knots through the air.

The airspeed indicator shows your speed through the air, not over the ground.

Answer 3: C) Your aircraft's relation to the horizon

The attitude indicator shows whether you're climbing, descending, or flying level.

Answer 4: C) East

A heading of 90 degrees means you're flying east.

CHAPTER 7: BLOCK COUNTING

Block Counting, while it may sound like child's play, is a subtest that can really test your spatial awareness and attention to detail. It's not just about counting blocks; it's about doing it quickly and accurately under time pressure. This skill is particularly useful in fields that require spatial reasoning and quick decision-making, like piloting an aircraft or planning tactical maneuvers.

The Basics: What You're Up Against

In the Block Counting subtest, you'll be presented with a series of three-dimensional arrangements of blocks. Your task is to count the number of blocks in each configuration. Sounds simple, right? Well, the catch is that some blocks may be partially or entirely hidden behind others. Your job is to mentally "move" these blocks around so you can count them all.

Strategies for Counting Blocks

1. Start from One Corner: Choose a corner and start your count from there. This gives you a reference point and makes it easier to keep track.
2. Use a Systematic Approach: Whether you go row by row or column by column, stick to a method. Consistency will help you avoid double-counting or missing blocks.
3. Chunking: If there are groups of blocks, count them as a single unit. For example, if you see a row of four blocks, think of it as "four" rather than counting each block individually.
4. Eliminate and Confirm: If you're unsure about a block, mentally remove it, complete your count, and then add it back in. This helps confirm its existence and your count.
5. Practice, Practice, Practice: The more you practice, the quicker and more accurate you'll become. It's all about training your brain to see and process these configurations efficiently.

This subtest measures your ability to visualize a three-dimensional stack of blocks and determine how many blocks are touching the numbered blocks. It also tests your ability to observe and deduce information that cannot be seen directly. Carefully study the way the blocks are stacked. Keep in mind that all of the blocks in a stack are the same size and shape.

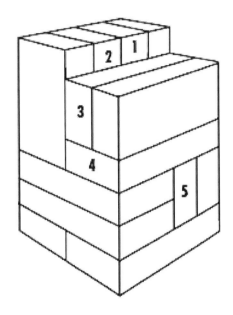

Question 1: How many blocks touch Block 1?

Question 2: How many blocks touch Block 2?

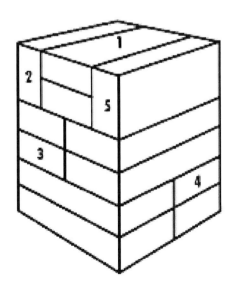

Question 3: How many blocks touch Block 1?

Question 4: How many blocks touch Block 2?

Question 5: How many blocks touch Block 3?

Question 6: How many blocks touch Block 4?

Question 7: How many blocks touch Block 5?

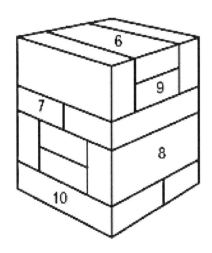

Question 8: How many blocks touch Block 6?

Question 9: How many blocks touch Block 7?

Question 10: How many blocks touch Block 8?

Question 11: How many blocks touch Block 9?

Question 12: How many blocks touch Block 10?

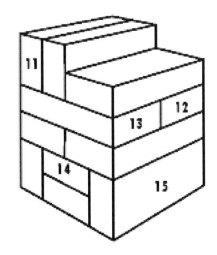

Question 13: How many blocks touch Block 11?

Question 14: How many blocks touch Block 12?

Question 15: How many blocks touch Block 13?

ANSWERS:

1. D 5
2. D 5
3. B 3 (Block 1 touches three blocks: one to the left, one below, & one to the right).
4. B 3 (Block 2 touches three blocks: one below, & two to the right).
5. C 4 (Block 3 touches four blocks: one above, one below, & two to the right).
6. C 4 (Block 4 touches four blocks: one above, one to the left, & two below).
7. B 3 (Block 5 touches three blocks: two to the left & one below).
8. B 3 (Block 6 touches three blocks: one to the left, one below, & one to the right).
9. E (Block 7 touches four blocks: one above, two below, & one to the right).
10. D (Block 8 touches five blocks: one above, two to the left, & two below).
11. D (Block 9 touches five blocks: one above, one to the left, two below, & one to the right).
12. C (Block 10 touches four blocks: three above & one to the right).
13. B (Block 11 touches three blocks: one below & two to the right).
14. E (Block 12 touches six blocks: three above, one to the left, & two below).
15. E (Block 13 touches six blocks: three above, two below, & one to the right).

CHAPTER 8: TABLE READING

Tables are everywhere, aren't they? From flight schedules to mission briefings, tables are a quick and efficient way to present a lot of information. But if you're not careful, they can also be a quick way to get lost in a sea of numbers and text. That's why this chapter is all about mastering the art of table reading.

Why Table Reading Matters

In the Air Force, you'll encounter tables more often than you might think. Whether it's a table showing different aircraft specifications or a timetable for troop deployments, being able to quickly interpret and make decisions based on table data is a skill you'll use again and again. And let's not forget, it's also a crucial part of the AFOQT!

The Basics: What to Look For

When you're faced with a table, the first thing to do is identify its components. Tables usually have a title, column headers, and rows. The title tells you what the table is about. Column headers indicate what each column represents, and the rows are where the actual data is.

Strategies for Quick Interpretation

1. Scan First, Read Later: Before diving into the details, give the table a quick scan. This will give you a general idea of what's where.
2. Identify Key Columns and Rows: Not all information in a table is equally important. Identify the key columns and rows that are most relevant to the question at hand.
3. Use Your Finger or a Pointer: This might sound old-school, but physically pointing to the information you're reading can significantly improve your focus and speed.
4. Practice, Practice, Practice: The more you practice, the quicker you'll get. So, don't shy away from those practice questions!

Practice Questions: Time to Shine

Alright, let's put these strategies to the test. Imagine a table that lists different types of aircraft, their maximum speed, and their range.

Model Number	Maximum Speed (mph)	Range (miles)
Airbus A380	565	9,800
Boeing 747-8	595	8,000
Boeing 787-10	560	7,400
Airbus A350-900	560	8,600
Boeing 777X	550	8,700
Airbus A321neo	540	4,000
Boeing 737 MAX 10	530	3,400
Airbus A330neo	525	8,100
Boeing 777-300ER	515	8,500
Airbus A350-1000	510	9,200
Boeing 787-9	510	8,400

Now, answer the following questions:

1. Which aircraft has the maximum range?
2. What is the maximum speed of Boeing 787-9?
3. How many aircraft have a range greater than 500 miles?

Remember, the goal here isn't just to find the right answer but to do it quickly and efficiently. Time yourself while answering these questions to get a sense of your speed.

Answers:

1. Boeing 747-8

2. 510 Mph

3. All

CHAPTER 9: AVIATION INFORMATION

Ah, aviation—the dream of soaring through the skies, feeling the wind rush past as you climb to new heights. But let's bring it back down to Earth for a moment. In the Air Force, understanding aviation isn't just a passion; it's a requirement. And that's where the Aviation Information subtest comes in.

Key Terms: Your Aviation Lexicon, Expanded

Altitude: More Than Just Heights

When we talk about altitude, we're not just talking about how high you are off the ground. In aviation, altitude is your vertical position relative to a specific reference, usually sea level. But here's the kicker: there are different types of altitude—true altitude, indicated altitude, and pressure altitude. Each serves a unique purpose. For instance, indicated altitude is what you read directly from the altimeter in the cockpit. It's your go-to for most in-flight operations.

Airspeed: It's All Relative

Airspeed isn't just how fast you're going; it's how fast you're going relative to the air around you. Think of it like walking on a moving sidewalk. Your speed relative to the ground (groundspeed) is your own walking speed plus the speed of the moving sidewalk. In aviation, we break airspeed down into:

- **Indicated Airspeed (IAS):** This is the speed you read on your cockpit instruments. It's crucial for safe flight maneuvers.
- **True Airspeed (TAS):** This is your actual speed through the air, corrected for altitude and temperature. It's like your "honest" speed, telling you how fast you're really going.
- **Groundspeed (GS):** This is your speed relative to the ground. It's TAS adjusted for wind speed and direction. Groundspeed is what counts when you're calculating how long your flight will take.

Lift: The Skyward Force

Lift is what makes flight possible. It's the force that opposes gravity and allows the aircraft to rise. But it's not just about going up; it's about how you go up. Lift depends on several factors, like wing shape, air density, and speed. The angle of the wings—known as the "angle of attack"—also plays a crucial role. Too steep an angle and you risk stalling the aircraft; too shallow, and you won't generate enough lift to take off.

The Four Forces of Flight: The Pillars of Aviation

Ah, the four musketeers of the sky—Lift, Gravity, Thrust, and Drag. These forces are like the ingredients in a perfect recipe for flight. Too much of one or too little of another, and you're not going anywhere.

Lift: The Skyward Force

You've probably experienced lift in its simplest form when you stick your hand out of a moving car window and angle it upward. Your hand rises, right? In aviation, lift is a bit more complex but follows the same principle. The shape of an aircraft's wings and the angle at which they meet the oncoming air (known as the angle of attack) are meticulously designed to maximize lift. When the aircraft speeds up, the wings slice through the air, creating a pressure difference that lifts the plane off the ground. It's like magic, but with physics.

Gravity: The Down-to-Earth Reality

Gravity is the party pooper at our flight fiesta. It's constantly pulling the aircraft toward Earth's center. But here's the thing: without gravity, we wouldn't need lift, and flight as we know it wouldn't exist. So, in a way, gravity is that challenging friend who makes you better, even if they're a bit of a downer sometimes. Pilots must always be aware of gravity's pull, especially during takeoff and landing, the most critical phases of flight.

Thrust: The Forward Momentum

Imagine you're on a skateboard. To move forward, you push off the ground with your foot—that's thrust. In an aircraft, thrust comes from the engines. Whether it's a propeller or a jet engine, the principle is the same: expel air backward to move forward. It's Newton's third law in action—every action has an equal and opposite reaction. Thrust must overcome drag and any opposing winds to keep the aircraft moving forward. It's the driving force that says, "Onward!"

Drag: The Invisible Hand

If thrust is telling you to go "Onward," drag is the one pulling your shirt from behind, saying, "Hold on a minute!" It's the aerodynamic resistance the aircraft faces as it moves through the air. Factors like air density, speed, and the aircraft's shape all contribute to drag. And just like you adjust your posture on that skateboard to minimize wind resistance, pilots and engineers make various adjustments to reduce drag, from the design phase all the way to in-flight maneuvers.

Types of Aircraft: Know Your Birds (Continued)

Ah, the beauty of flight! From the majestic jumbo jets that grace our skies to the nimble helicopters that can hover in place, each type of aircraft is a marvel of engineering.

- **Jumbo Jets:** These are the titans of the sky, capable of carrying hundreds of passengers across continents. Think Boeing 747 or the Airbus A380. They're like the cruise ships of the air—spacious, luxurious, and built for long-haul flights

- **Helicopters:** The gymnasts of aviation. These guys can take off and land vertically, hover, and even fly backward if needed. They're versatile and are often used for specialized tasks like search and rescue, medical evacuations, and yes, even traffic reports.

- **Drones:** The newcomers on the block. These unmanned aircraft are making waves in everything from photography to agriculture. They're like the Swiss Army knives of the aviation world—small but incredibly versatile.

- **Fighter Jets:** These are the speedsters, built for agility and armed to the teeth. Think F-16s or MiGs. They're the ones you'll see doing incredible acrobatics at air shows and are crucial for defense and tactical missions.

- **Propeller Planes:** The classics never go out of style. These aircraft are generally smaller and are often used for training new pilots, short-haul flights, or even just for the sheer joy of flying.

- **Gliders:** These are the minimalists of the aviation world. No engines, just wings and a prayer. They're towed into the air and then released to glide gracefully back to Earth, carried by air currents.

CHAPTER 10: GENERAL SCIENCE

Science is not just a subject; it's a way of understanding the world around us. Whether you're gazing at the stars, mixing chemicals in a lab, or observing the intricate patterns of a leaf, science offers a lens to see the intricacies of the universe. In this chapter, we'll explore the essential scientific principles you'll need to grasp for the AFOQT's General Science subtest. We'll delve into physics, chemistry, and biology, breaking down complex theories into bite-sized, understandable pieces.

Physics: The Laws of Motion - A Closer Look

Ah, Newton's laws of motion. They're like the golden rules of how things move and interact in the universe. These laws are the reason you can predict where a thrown ball will land or why you feel pushed back into your seat when your car accelerates.

First Law: The Law of Inertia

Think about sitting in a parked car. You're not going anywhere, right? That's inertia in action. Your body wants to stay at rest. Now, if the car suddenly starts moving, you feel pushed back against the seat. Again, that's inertia, but this time it's your body's resistance to the change in motion. It's like your body is saying, "Hey, I was comfortable; why the sudden move?"

Second Law: F=ma (Force Equals Mass Times Acceleration)

This one's a bit like a recipe: Force is the product of mass and acceleration. Imagine you're pushing a sled. The heavier the sled, the harder you have to push (apply force) to make it move (accelerate). If the sled is packed with bricks (increased mass), you're going to have to push even harder (more force) to get the same speed (acceleration). It's like the universe's way of saying, "You want to change something? Well, here's the cost."

Third Law: Action and Reaction

This law is the reason rockets fly and why you move backward when you shoot a basketball. When you jump off a diving board, your legs push down on the board (action), and the board pushes you up into the air (reaction). It's a cosmic give-and-take that happens in an instant but has everlasting implications.

Universality of These Laws

What's truly mind-blowing is that these laws aren't just Earthly concepts; they're universal truths. Whether you're floating in the zero-gravity abyss of space or standing on the peak of Mount Everest, these laws apply. They're like the universe's operating manual, written in a language that transcends time and space.

Chemistry: The Building Blocks of Matter

Ah, chemistry, the subject that brings to mind colorful liquids, mysterious reactions, and, of course, the periodic table. It's like the universe's recipe book, detailing what everything is made of and how it all interacts.

Atoms: The Cosmic LEGO Blocks

Think of atoms as the universe's LEGO blocks. They're the tiniest units that make up all matter, and just like LEGOs, they come in different types—118 to be exact, each one a different element. An atom itself is a fascinating little entity, made up of protons, neutrons, and electrons.

- Protons: Positively charged particles found in the nucleus.
- Neutrons: Neutral particles that also reside in the nucleus.
- Electrons: Negatively charged particles that orbit the nucleus.

These subatomic particles are like the members of a tiny cosmic family, each playing its role to keep the atom stable.

Molecules: When Atoms Team Up

If atoms are individual LEGO blocks, then molecules are the structures you build with them. A molecule is formed when two or more atoms join forces, usually by sharing electrons. This is where the magic happens—oxygen atoms bonding with hydrogen atoms to create water, carbon atoms linking up with oxygen to form carbon dioxide, and so on.

- Covalent Bonds: Atoms share electrons.
- Ionic Bonds: One atom gives an electron to another.

The type of bond affects the molecule's properties, like how water is a liquid at room temperature, but methane is a gas.

Chemical Reactions: The Universe's Dance Moves

Life is a series of chemical reactions. When you breathe, eat, or even fall in love, atoms and molecules are at play. In a chemical reaction, atoms rearrange themselves to create new substances. This can happen in various ways:

- Synthesis: Two or more substances combine to form a new one.

- Decomposition: A single substance breaks down into two or more substances.

- Replacement: One element in a compound is replaced by another.

Imagine baking a cake. You start with individual ingredients like flour, sugar, and eggs—each one a different "compound." Mix them together, apply some heat, and voila! You've got yourself a cake—a delicious result of chemical reactions.

Biology: The Study of Life

Ah, biology—the study of life, in all its wondrous forms. From the tiniest microorganisms to the towering redwoods, life is a complex tapestry woven from cells and DNA.

Cells: The Basic Unit of Life

Think of cells as the bricks and mortar of all living things. Whether it's a simple, single-celled organism like bacteria or a complex, multicellular organism like a human, cells are the foundational units that make life possible.

- **Prokaryotic Cells:** These are your straightforward, no-nonsense cells. Found in bacteria and archaea, they don't have a nucleus or other membrane-bound organelles. But don't underestimate them; they've been around for billions of years!

- **Eukaryotic Cells:** These are the divas of the cellular world, complete with a nucleus and specialized structures called organelles. You'll find these cells in plants, animals, and fungi.

It's like a bustling city where each cell has a specific job, from energy production in the mitochondria to waste management in the lysosomes. Understanding how cells function and interact is crucial, not just for biology but for understanding life itself.

DNA: The Blueprint of Life

If cells are the bricks, then DNA is the blueprint. It's a long, winding molecule that holds the instructions for building and maintaining an organism. Imagine it as a cookbook written in a four-letter alphabet (A, T, C, G), where each 'recipe' is a specific gene.

- Genes: These are specific sequences of DNA that determine particular traits, like the color of your eyes or your ability to roll your tongue.
- Chromosomes: Think of these as chapters in the cookbook, each holding multiple recipes (genes). Humans typically have 23 pairs of chromosomes.
- Genome: This is the entire cookbook, cover to cover. It's the full set of genetic instructions that make you, well, you.

DNA isn't just about heredity; it's also about function. It tells cells what proteins to make and when, essentially guiding the cell's daily operations.

CHAPTER 11: READING COMPREHENSION

Reading comprehension isn't just about understanding words on a page; it's a skill that's deeply ingrained in an officer's Professional Military Education (PME). Whether you're reading orders, interpreting intelligence reports, or studying for further qualifications, your ability to comprehend written material is crucial. So, let's not underestimate this section of the AFOQT—it's more than a test; it's a preview of what's to come in your military career.

Types of Passages You'll Encounter: A Closer Look

When you sit down to tackle the Reading Comprehension section, you'll find that not all passages are created equal. Some will be narrative, drawing you into a story or recounting an event in a way that feels almost like you're there. These passages often test your ability to understand sequences of events, motivations, or emotional nuances.

Then there are the expository passages. These are more straightforward but can be dense. They aim to inform or explain, often throwing a lot of facts or technical jargon your way. Here, you'll likely be tested on your ability to grasp complex information, identify key points, and understand the logical flow of ideas.

Understanding the type of passage, you're dealing with can help you tailor your reading strategy. For narrative texts, you might focus on character motivations or the sequence of events. For expository texts, you'll want to zero in on key terms and main ideas. Either way, your goal is to extract as much useful information as possible in the time you have.

Strategies for Effective Reading: Skimming and Scanning Unpacked

So, you're staring at a dense paragraph with the clock ticking down. What do you do? This is where skimming and scanning come into play, two techniques that are as practical as they are effective.

Skimming is like flying over a city in a helicopter. You get a bird's-eye view, enough to identify the main landmarks but not so much the tiny details. When you skim, you're running your eyes over the text to capture the essence of the passage. You're looking for main ideas, topic sentences, or any words that are repeated or emphasized. This gives you a framework to understand the more detailed questions that might come later.

Scanning is a bit different. Imagine you've lost your keys and you're scanning the room to find them. Your eyes dart around, ignoring everything that isn't a key. Similarly, when you scan a passage, you're looking for specific information—a name, a date, a term. You're not interested in understanding the entire passage; you're focused on finding that one piece of information that will answer the question at hand.

Understanding implied content

Understanding implied content is like being a detective of the written word. You're not just absorbing information; you're actively engaging with it, asking questions, and making inferences. This skill is invaluable, especially in high-stakes environments like the military, where a single misunderstanding can have significant consequences.

Imagine you're reading a passage about a historical military operation. The text might not explicitly state the challenges faced by the troops, but it might describe harsh weather conditions, limited supplies, and a tight timeline. From these details, you can infer that the operation was fraught with logistical difficulties, even if the text doesn't say so outright. This ability to "read between the lines" is what understanding implied content is all about.

When you're practicing for the AFOQT, don't just focus on the literal meaning of the text. Consider the tone, the choice of words, and even what's deliberately left unsaid. For example, if a passage describes a pilot carefully checking every gauge before takeoff but doesn't specifically say why, you can infer that meticulous attention to detail is crucial for flight safety.

This skill is not just about answering test questions correctly; it's a critical thinking skill that you'll use throughout your military career. Whether you're interpreting orders, reading intelligence reports, or analyzing strategic documents, understanding implied content will help you make more informed decisions.

So, the next time you're practicing, challenge yourself. Don't just look for the obvious; delve deeper. Try to uncover the hidden layers of meaning in the text. The more you practice this skill, the more intuitive it will become, and the better prepared you'll be, not just for the AFOQT but for the complex, nuanced tasks you'll encounter as an officer.

The Role of Vocabulary

Another aspect that often goes unnoticed but plays a significant role in reading comprehension is vocabulary. Knowing the meaning of words, especially those that are less common, can be a game-changer. It's not just about understanding the words in the questions but also grasping the nuances in the passages you'll read. A strong vocabulary can help you quickly understand the context, saving you valuable time during the test.

Context Clues: Your Silent Helper

Sometimes you'll come across words or phrases that you're not familiar with, and that's okay. The ability to use context clues is invaluable in these situations. The surrounding sentences can often give you a good idea of what an unfamiliar word or phrase means. This skill is particularly useful when dealing with technical or military jargon that you might not have encountered before.

The Importance of Focus and Concentration

Reading comprehension is not just about your ability to understand text; it's also about your ability to focus. Distractions can easily throw you off, leading to mistakes that could have been avoided. Techniques such as deep breathing or briefly closing your eyes can help you regain your focus during the test. Remember, every second counts, so maintaining a high level of concentration is crucial.

Sample Passage

Sample Passage 1: The Solar System

The solar system consists of the Sun and the celestial objects gravitationally bound in orbit around it, including eight planets and their moons, as well as asteroids, meteoroids, and comets. While the Sun holds 99.8% of the solar system's mass, the planets—chiefly Jupiter and Saturn—hold the rest.

Question 1: What does the solar system primarily consist of?

A) The Sun and the Moon

B) The Sun and celestial objects

C) Jupiter and Saturn

D) Asteroids and comets

Answer: B) The Sun and celestial objects

Explanation: The passage clearly states that the solar system consists of the Sun and celestial objects gravitationally bound in orbit around it. Option B is the most accurate answer.

Sample Passage 2: Leadership Qualities

Effective leadership is not about making speeches or being liked; leadership is defined by results, not attributes. Good leaders foster a team environment where each member feels empowered, valued, and heard.

Question 2: According to the passage, what defines effective leadership?

A) Making speeches

B) Being liked

C) Results

D) Attributes

Answer: C) Results

Explanation: The passage explicitly states that effective leadership is defined by results, not attributes. Therefore, option C is the correct answer.

Sample Passage 3: Environmental Conservation

Conserving the environment is not just an ethical responsibility but also a necessity for human survival. Pollution, deforestation, and climate change are all human-made problems that require immediate attention.

Question 3: What is the main point of the passage?

A) Pollution is a human-made problem.

B) Conserving the environment is an ethical responsibility.

C) Human survival depends on environmental conservation.

D) Climate change requires immediate attention.

Answer: C) Human survival depends on environmental conservation

Explanation: While the passage mentions several issues like pollution and climate change, its main point is that conserving the environment is a necessity for human survival. Option C captures this idea best.

CHAPTER 12: SITUATIONAL JUDGMENT

Situational Judgment Tests (SJTs) are designed to assess your ability to handle various interpersonal situations that you're likely to encounter as an officer in the Air Force. These tests are not just another hurdle to jump over; they are a critical evaluation tool that can give insight into your decision-making, problem-solving, and leadership skills. Understanding the nuances of these tests can be your secret weapon in not just passing but excelling in this section of the AFOQT.

Why Situational Judgment Tests Matter

You might wonder, "Why do I need to prove my situational judgment skills?" The answer is simple: Officers are often faced with complex scenarios that require quick thinking, ethical decision-making, and effective communication. Your ability to navigate these situations can significantly impact not only your career but also the lives of those you lead.

Types of Scenarios You Might Face

In this section of the AFOQT, you'll encounter a variety of scenarios that test your skills in:

1. Conflict Resolution: How do you handle disagreements among team members?
2. Team Dynamics: Can you foster a positive and productive environment?
3. Ethical Dilemmas: What do you do when faced with a morally ambiguous situation?

A Step-by-Step Approach to Analyzing Situations

When you're presented with a scenario, it's easy to jump to conclusions or make snap judgments. However, a more methodical approach can yield better results. Here's a simple guide to help you:

1. **Understand the Context:** Before making any decisions, grasp the situation's background and the involved parties.
2. **Identify the Problem:** Clearly define what issue needs to be resolved.
3. **Evaluate Possible Solutions:** Weigh the pros and cons of each potential action.

Practice Scenarios

Let's dive into some practice scenarios to get a feel for what you might encounter.

Scenario 1: Team Conflict

Your team is divided on how to approach a project. Half want to use Method A, and the other half insist on Method B.

Question: What is the best course of action?

A) Choose Method A without discussion.

B) Choose Method B without discussion.

C) Facilitate a team discussion to reach a consensus.

D) Decide on your own and inform the team later.

Answer: C) Facilitate a team discussion to reach a consensus.

Explanation: The best course of action is to involve the team in the decision-making process. This not only resolves the issue but also fosters a sense of ownership and unity among team members.

CHAPTER 13: ROTATED BLOCKS

The Rotated Blocks subtest is one of the more unique sections of the Air Force Officer Qualifying Test (AFOQT). Unlike other subtests that focus on verbal or mathematical skills, this one challenges your spatial awareness and ability to visualize objects in different orientations. This skill is crucial for various roles in the Air Force, especially for those involving navigation, piloting, or any tasks requiring a keen sense of spatial relationships.

Understanding the Rotated Blocks Subtest

In this subtest, you'll be presented with a series of blocks that have been rotated to various degrees. Your task is to identify which blocks match the original figure. It may sound simple, but under the pressure of time and amidst the stress of the test, it can become challenging.

What You'll Encounter

A series of questions, each featuring a 'target' block.

Multiple-choice options showing the target block rotated to different degrees.

A time limit, making speed and accuracy essential.

Strategies for Success

1. Visualize the Axis of Rotation

Imagine a line running through the center of the block. As you look at the answer choices, visualize this line and how the block would look if rotated around it. This mental exercise can help you quickly identify the correct block.

2. Use Elimination

Often, you'll find that some options can be immediately eliminated because they are mirror images or have a different configuration than the target block. Narrowing down your choices can save you precious seconds.

Practice Questions

Examine the two blocks presented below. Despite their differing orientations, the blocks are identical.

          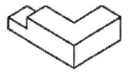

Observe the two blocks presented below. They are distinct and cannot be rotated or manipulated to appear identical.

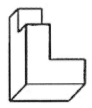   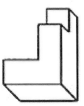

a. Now look at sample question S1 below. Which of the five choices is just like the first block?

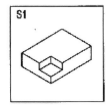  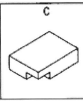 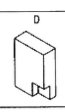 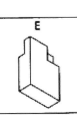

b. Now look at sample questions S2 and S3 below.

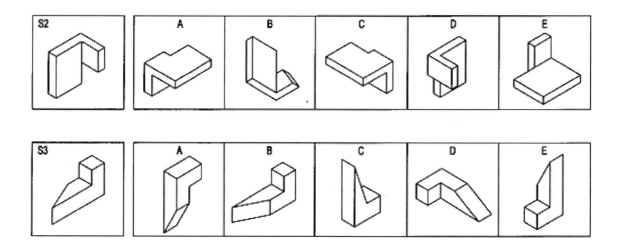

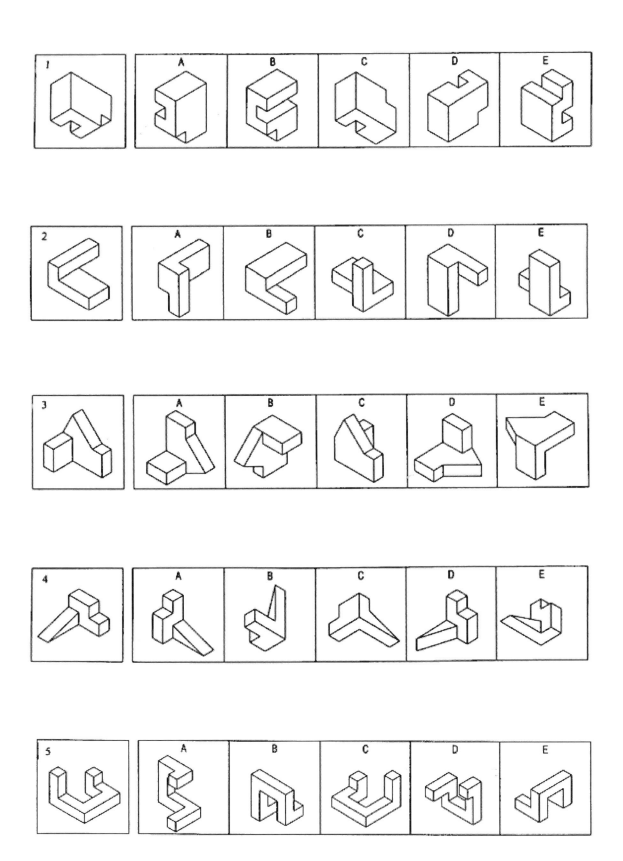

a.

The correct answer is D. It is the same block placed in a different position.

b.

The correct answer for S2 is C. The correct answer for S3 is A.

1. A

2. B

3. D

4. C

5. B

CHAPTER 14: HIDDEN FIGURES

The Hidden Figures subtest is a fascinating yet challenging part of the Air Force Officer Qualifying Test (AFOQT). Unlike other sections that test your verbal or mathematical abilities, this one delves into your attention to detail and pattern recognition skills. It's a crucial skill set for various roles in the Air Force, particularly those that require keen observational abilities.

Understanding the Hidden Figures Subtest

In this subtest, you'll be presented with complex figures containing smaller, hidden shapes. Your task is to identify these hidden shapes within a given time limit. The challenge lies not just in recognizing the shapes but also in doing so quickly and accurately.

What to Expect

A series of complex figures, each containing one or more hidden shapes.

Multiple-choice questions asking you to identify the hidden shape.

A time constraint that adds an element of pressure to the task.

Strategies for Success

1. Scan the Perimeter

Start by scanning the outer edges of the complex figure. Often, the hidden shapes are tucked away in corners or along the sides. A quick perimeter scan can help you locate these shapes more efficiently.

2. Break it Down

If the figure is particularly complex, try breaking it down into smaller sections in your mind. Focus on one section at a time to identify the hidden shape. This approach makes the task more manageable and less overwhelming.

3. Use Reference Points

Look for unique lines, angles, or intersections within the complex figure that can serve as reference points. These can guide you to the location of the hidden shape.

4. Practice Mindfulness

Stay present and focused. The more you let your mind wander, the harder it will be to spot the hidden figures. Mindfulness techniques, such as deep breathing, can help maintain your focus.

Practice Questions

Instructions: This section of the test assesses your skill in identifying a basic shape within a more intricate design. At the top of each page, you'll find five shapes labeled with letters. Following these, each page features multiple drawings numbered sequentially. Your task is to discern which lettered shape is embedded within each numbered drawing.

The lettered shapes are:

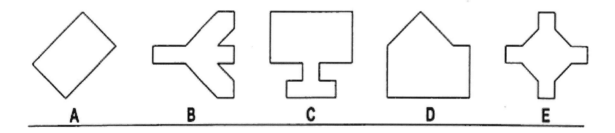

The numbered drawings are like drawing X below. Which one of the five figures is contained in drawing X?

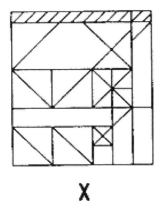

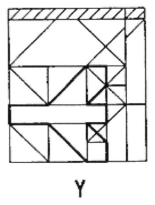

X

Y

In drawing X, figure B is embedded, making B the correct answer for sample question X. Drawing Y is identical to drawing X, except that figure B's outline is emphasized to indicate its full presence in the drawing. The figure maintains the same dimensions and location as it does at the top of the page, eliminating the need to rotate the page to identify it. For each numbered drawing, determine which lettered figure is included within it.

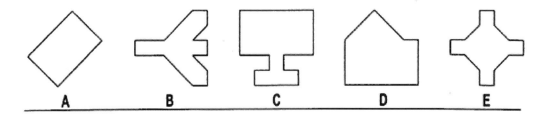

A   B   C   D   E

1

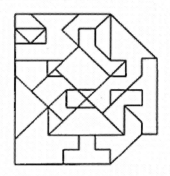

4

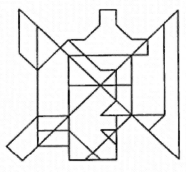

2

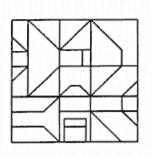

5

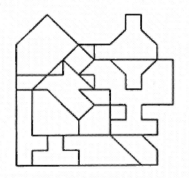

3

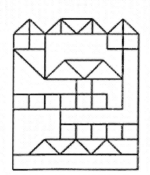

Answers:

1. A

2. B

3. C

4. B

5. D

CHAPTER 15: PRACTICE TEST Q&A

Verbal Analogies

1. Book : Author :: Song : ?

A) Singer

B) Composer

C) Instrument

D) Lyrics

2. Square : Quadrilateral :: Circle : ?

A) Sphere

B) Ellipse

C) Oval

D) Shape

3. Tree : Forest :: Fish : ?

A) Water

B) School

C) Pond

D) Aquarium

4. Pen : Write :: Scissors : ?

A) Cut

B) Open

C) Hold

D) Sharp

5. Apple : Fruit :: Oak : ?

A) Wood

B) Tree

C) Leaf

D) Forest

6. Hot : Cold :: Brave : ?

A) Courageous

B) Cowardly

C) Fearful

D) Bold

7. Moon : Lunar :: Sun : ?

A) Solar

B) Stellar

C) Planetary

D) Celestial

8. Car : Garage :: Boat : ?

A) Water

B) Dock

C) Marina

D) Shipyard

9. Finger : Hand :: Toe : ?

A) Leg

B) Foot

C) Ankle

D) Nail

10. Bread : Bakery :: Books : ?

A) Library

B) Bookstore

C) School

D) Author

11. Dog : Kennel :: Chicken : ?

A) Farm

B) Coop

C) Nest

D) Barn

12. Water : Liquid :: Ice : ?

A) Cold

B) Solid

C) Frozen

D) Melt

13. King : Throne :: Student : ?

A) School

B) Desk

C) Class

D) Teacher

14. Paint : Artist :: Words : ?

A) Writer

B) Speaker

C) Reader

D) Listener

15. Fire : Hot :: Snow : ?

A) Cold

B) White

C) Wet

D) Slippery

16. Knife : Cut :: Hammer : ?

A) Build

B) Pound

C) Break

D) Nail

17. Salt : Sodium :: Water : ?

A) Hydrogen

B) Liquid

C) H2O

D) Oxygen

18. Money : Wallet :: Cards : ?

A) Game

B) Deck

C) Hand

D) Purse

19. Eyes : See :: Ears : ?

A) Listen

B) Hear

C) Sound

D) Noise

20. Car : Fuel :: Human : ?

A) Water

B) Food

C) Air

D) Exercise

21. Bird : Fly :: Fish : ?

A) Swim

B) Water

C) Breathe

D) Dive

22. Day : Night :: Full : ?

A) Empty

B) Half

C) Dark

D) Light

23. River : Stream :: Mountain : ?

A) Hill

B) Rock

C) Valley

D) Cliff

24. Coffee : Caffeine :: Wine : ?

A) Alcohol

B) Grapes

C) Glass

D) Vineyard

25. Pencil : Eraser :: Knife : ?

A) Blade

B) Sharpener

C) Handle

D) Cut

26. Teacher : Classroom :: Doctor : ?

A) Hospital

B) Clinic

C) Office

D) Patient

27. Winter : Snow :: Summer : ?

A) Sun

B) Heat

C) Beach

D) Ice cream

28. Cat : Feline :: Dog : ?

A) Canine

B) Mammal

C) Pet

D) Animal

29. Earth : Planet :: Moon : ?

A) Star

B) Satellite

C) Universe

D) Solar System

30. Smile : Happy :: Frown : ?

A) Sad

B) Angry

C) Confused

D) Serious

31. Car : Road :: Train : ?

A) Station

B) Track

C) Tunnel

D) Platform

32. Computer : Software :: Brain : ?

A) Hardware

B) Mind

C) Intelligence

D) Memory

33. Apple : Orchard :: Grape : ?

A) Vineyard

B) Garden

C) Farm

D) Market

34. Clock : Time :: Thermometer : ?

A) Heat

B) Temperature

C) Weather

D) Degrees

35. Lion : Roar :: Snake : ?

A) Slither

B) Hiss

C) Bite

D) Crawl

36. Bread : Yeast :: Cake : ?

A) Flour

B) Sugar

C) Baking Powder

D) Oven

37. Ship : Sea :: Airplane : ?

A) Sky

B) Runway

C) Airport

D) Clouds

38. Money : Bank :: Data : ?

A) Computer

B) Server

C) Internet

D) Cloud

39. Eyes : Vision :: Nose : ?

A) Smell

B) Breathe

C) Sneeze

D) Nostrils

40. Chair : Sit :: Bed : ?

A) Sleep

B) Rest

C) Furniture

D) Room

41. Paint : Canvas :: Ink : ?

A) Pen

B) Paper

C) Printer

D) Quill

42. Phone : Call :: Camera : ?

A) Picture

B) Lens

C) Flash

D) Zoom

43. Book : Read :: Music : ?

A) Listen

B) Play

C) Dance

D) Sing

44. Rain : Wet :: Wind : ?

A) Dry

B) Blow

C) Air

D) Cool

45. Ocean : Saltwater :: Lake : ?

A) Freshwater

B) Pond

C) River

D) Sea

46. Sugar : Sweet :: Lemon : ?

A) Sour

B) Citrus

C) Yellow

D) Fruit

47. Car : Gasoline :: Electric Car : ?

A) Battery

B) Electricity

C) Plug

D) Solar

48. Athlete : Stadium :: Actor : ?

A) Movie

B) Theater

C) Stage

D) Audience

49. Night : Dark :: Day : ?

A) Light

B) Bright

C) Morning

D) Sun

50. Elephant : Trunk :: Kangaroo : ?

A) Tail

B) Pouch

C) Jump

D) Australia

51. Rain : Umbrella :: Sun : ?

A) Sunglasses

B) Hat

C) Sunscreen

D) Beach

52. Flower : Petal :: Tree : ?

A) Leaf

B) Bark

C) Branch

D) Root

53. Clock : Hour :: Calendar : ?

A) Day

B) Week

C) Month

D) Year

54. Shoes : Feet :: Gloves : ?

A) Hands

B) Fingers

C) Arms

D) Wrist

55. Air : Breathe :: Food : ?

A) Eat

B) Cook

C) Taste

D) Digest

56. Bird : Nest :: Bee : ?

A) Hive

B) Honey

C) Flower

D) Buzz

57. Water : Thirst :: Food : ?

A) Hunger

B) Taste

C) Nutrition

D) Meal

58. Pen : Ink :: Pencil : ?

A) Lead

B) Wood

C) Eraser

D) Graphite

59. Baby : Crib :: Patient : ?

A) Hospital

B) Bed

C) Doctor

D) Medicine

60. Book : Chapter :: Movie : ?

A) Scene

B) Act

C) Frame

D) Sequel

61. Fire : Extinguisher :: Cut : ?

A) Scissors

B) Bandage

C) Knife

D) Wound

62. Car : Drive :: Bicycle : ?

A) Pedal

B) Ride

C) Wheel

D) Cycle

63. Sun : Solar :: Moon : ?

A) Lunar

B) Celestial

C) Night

D) Tide

64. Apple : Orchard :: Cow : ?

A) Farm

B) Barn

C) Pasture

D) Dairy

65. Paint : Wall :: Nail : ?

A) Hammer

B) Wood

C) Screw

D) Board

66. Teacher : Student :: Employer : ?

A) Job

B) Employee

C) Work

D) Office

67. Fish : Swim :: Bird : ?

A) Fly

B) Nest

C) Feather

D) Sing

68. Library : Books :: Museum : ?

A) Paintings

B) History

C) Artifacts

D) Visitors

69. Candle : Wax :: Pencil : ?

A) Wood

B) Lead

C) Graphite

D) Eraser

70. Chef : Kitchen :: Mechanic : ?

A) Car

B) Garage

C) Tools

D) Engine

71. Moon : Night :: Sun : ?

A) Day

B) Morning

C) Sky

D) Solar

72. Shoes : Walk :: Glasses : ?

A) See

B) Read

C) Wear

D) Frame

73. Dog : Bark :: Cat : ?

A) Meow

B) Purr

C) Claw

D) Whiskers

74. Rain : Clouds :: Snow : ?

A) Winter

B) Cold

C) Sky

D) Ice

75. Apple : Red :: Banana : ?

A) Yellow

B) Fruit

C) Peel

D) Tropical

76. Car : Wheels :: Boat : ?

A) Sails

B) Anchor

C) Paddle

D) Hull

77. Money : Wallet :: ID : ?

A) Pocket

B) Purse

C) Cardholder

D) License

78. Tree : Oxygen :: Sun : ?

A) Light

B) Heat

C) Solar

D) Energy

79. Football : Touchdown :: Basketball : ?

A) Hoop

B) Dunk

C) Basket

D) Court

80. Lion : Pride :: Fish : ?

A) School

B) Swarm

C) Pod

D) Shoal

81. Coffee : Hot :: Ice Cream : ?

A) Cold

B) Sweet

C) Creamy

D) Frozen

82. Phone : Text :: Computer : ?

A) Email

B) Browse

C) Type

D) Search

83. Hammer : Nail :: Screwdriver : ?

A) Bolt

B) Screw

C) Wrench

D) Wood

84. Bread : Toast :: Milk : ?

A) Cheese

B) Cream

C) Yogurt

D) Butter

85. Car : Fuel :: Plant : ?

A) Sunlight

B) Water

C) Soil

D) Nutrients

86. Writer : Pen :: Painter : ?

A) Canvas

B) Brush

C) Palette

D) Easel

87. Water : Liquid :: Diamond : ?

A) Gem

B) Solid

C) Carbon

D) Jewelry

88. Teacher : Educate :: Doctor : ?

A) Heal

B) Prescribe

C) Diagnose

D) Consult

89. Ice : Cold :: Fire : ?

A) Hot

B) Burn

C) Flame

D) Ash

90. Tree : Forest :: Fish : ?

A) Ocean

B) Pond

C) River

D) Aquarium

91. Pen : Write :: Scissors : ?

A) Cut

B) Open

C) Sharp

D) Blade

92. Book : Author :: Song : ?

A) Singer

B) Composer

C) Lyricist

D) Musician

93. Sun : Day :: Moon : ?

A) Night

B) Lunar

C) Eclipse

D) Orbit

94. Car : Garage :: Airplane : ?

A) Airport

B) Hangar

C) Runway

D) Sky

95. Water : Drink :: Food : ?

A) Eat

B) Chew

C) Digest

D) Cook

96. Dog : Kennel :: Horse : ?

A) Stable

B) Farm

C) Pasture

D) Barn

97. Clock : Time :: Scale : ?

A) Weight

B) Balance

C) Measurement

D) Height

98. Apple : Fruit :: Oak : ?

A) Tree

B) Wood

C) Leaf

D) Acorn

99. Hammer : Carpenter :: Stethoscope : ?

A) Doctor

B) Nurse

C) Surgeon

D) Medical

100. Eyes : See :: Ears : ?

A) Hear

B) Listen

C) Sound

D) Earlobe

101. Bread : Bakery :: Books : ?

A) Library

B) Bookstore

C) Publisher

D) Author

102. Car : Fuel :: Human : ?

A) Food

B) Water

C) Oxygen

D) Energy

103. Paint : Artist :: Words : ?

A) Writer

B) Speaker

C) Poet

D) Orator

104. Rain : Wet :: Sun : ?

A) Dry

B) Hot

C) Bright

D) Warm

105. Shoes : Feet :: Hat : ?

A) Head

B) Hair

C) Cap

D) Ears

106. Money : Bank :: Information : ?

A) Internet

B) Library

C) Database

D) Encyclopedia

107. Fish : Fins :: Bird : ?

A) Feathers

B) Beak

C) Wings

D) Talons

108. Car : Drive :: Boat : ?

A) Sail

B) Row

C) Float

D) Anchor

109. Teacher : School :: Soldier : ?

A) Army

B) Barracks

C) Battlefield

D) War

110. Water : River :: Lava : ?

A) Volcano

B) Mountain

C) Magma

D) Crater

VA ANSWERS AND EXPLANATIONS

1. B) Composer - An author writes a book, and a composer writes a song.

2. B) Ellipse - A square is a type of quadrilateral, and a circle is a type of ellipse.

3. B) School - A tree is part of a forest, and a fish is part of a school.

4. A) Cut - A pen is used to write, and scissors are used to cut.

5. B) Tree - An apple is a type of fruit, and an oak is a type of tree.

6. B) Cowardly - Hot is the opposite of cold, and brave is the opposite of cowardly.

7. A) Solar - Moon relates to lunar, and sun relates to solar.

8. B) Dock - A car is stored in a garage, and a boat is stored at a dock.

9. B) Foot - A finger is part of a hand, and a toe is part of a foot.

10. B) Bookstore - Bread is sold in a bakery, and books are sold in a bookstore.

11. B) Coop - A dog stays in a kennel, and a chicken stays in a coop.

12. B) Solid - Water is a liquid, and ice is a solid.

13. B) Desk - A king sits on a throne, and a student sits at a desk.

14. A) Writer - An artist uses paint, and a writer uses words.

15. A) Cold - Fire is hot, and snow is cold.

16. B) Pound - A knife is used to cut, and a hammer is used to pound.

17. C) H2O - Salt is composed of sodium, and water is composed of H2O.

18. D) Purse - Money is kept in a wallet, and cards can be kept in a purse.

19. B) Hear - Eyes are used to see, and ears are used to hear.

20. B) Food - A car runs on fuel, and a human runs on food.

21. A) Swim - A bird flies, and a fish swims.

22. A) Empty - Day is the opposite of night, and full is the opposite of empty.

23. A) Hill - A river is a larger form of a stream, and a mountain is a larger form of a hill.

24. A) Alcohol - Coffee contains caffeine, and wine contains alcohol.

25. B) Sharpener - A pencil has an eraser for correcting mistakes, and a knife has a sharpener for honing its blade.

26. B) Clinic - A teacher works in a classroom, and a doctor works in a clinic.

27. B) Heat - Winter is associated with snow, and summer is associated with heat.

28. A) Canine - Cat belongs to the feline family, and dog belongs to the canine family.

29. B) Satellite - Earth is a planet, and Moon is a satellite.

30. A) Sad - A smile is an expression of happiness, and a frown is an expression of sadness.

31. B) Track - A car runs on a road, and a train runs on a track.

32. B) Mind - A computer runs on software, and the brain runs on the mind.

33. A) Vineyard - Apples are grown in an orchard, and grapes are grown in a vineyard.

34. B) Temperature - A clock measures time, and a thermometer measures temperature.

35. B) Hiss - A lion roars, and a snake hisses.

36. C) Baking Powder - Bread rises due to yeast, and cake rises due to baking powder.

37. A) Sky - A ship sails on the sea, and an airplane flies in the sky.

38. B) Server - Money is stored in a bank, and data is stored on a server.

39. A) Smell - Eyes are used for vision, and the nose is used for smell.

40. A) Sleep - A chair is used for sitting, and a bed is used for sleeping.

41. B) Paper - Paint is applied to canvas, and ink is applied to paper.

42. A) Picture - A phone is used for making calls, and a camera is used for taking pictures.

43. A) Listen - Books are for reading, and music is for listening.

44. D) Cool - Rain makes things wet, and wind makes things cool.

45. A) Freshwater - Oceans contain saltwater, and lakes contain freshwater.

46. A) Sour - Sugar is sweet, and lemon is sour.

47. A) Battery - A car runs on gasoline, and an electric car runs on a battery.

48. C) Stage - An athlete performs in a stadium, and an actor performs on a stage.

49. A) Light - Night is dark, and day is light.

50. B) Pouch - An elephant has a trunk, and a kangaroo has a pouch.

51. A) Sunglasses - An umbrella is used for rain, and sunglasses are used for sun.

52. A) Leaf - A flower has petals, and a tree has leaves.

53. A) Day - A clock measures hours, and a calendar measures days.

54. A) Hands - Shoes are worn on feet, and gloves are worn on hands.

55. A) Eat - We breathe air, and we eat food.

56. A) Hive - A bird lives in a nest, and a bee lives in a hive.

57. A) Hunger - Water quenches thirst, and food satisfies hunger.

58. D) Graphite - A pen uses ink, and a pencil uses graphite.

59. B) Bed - A baby sleeps in a crib, and a patient rests in a bed.

60. A) Scene - A book is divided into chapters, and a movie is divided into scenes.

61. B) Bandage - A fire is put out with an extinguisher, and a cut is covered with a bandage.

62. A) Pedal - You drive a car, and you pedal a bicycle.

63. A) Lunar - Sun is related to solar, and moon is related to lunar.

64. C) Pasture - Apples are grown in an orchard, and cows graze in a pasture.

65. D) Board - Paint is applied to a wall, and a nail is hammered into a board.

66. B) Employee - A teacher instructs students, and an employer hires employees.

67. A) Fly - Fish swim, and birds fly.

68. C) Artifacts - A library houses books, and a museum house artifacts.

69. C) Graphite - A candle is made of wax, and a pencil is made of graphite.

70. B) Garage - A chef works in a kitchen, and a mechanic works in a garage.

71. A) Day - The moon is associated with night, and the sun is associated with day.

72. A) See - Shoes are used to walk, and glasses are used to see.

73. A) Meow - A dog barks, and a cat meows.

74. C) Sky - Rain comes from clouds, and snow comes from the sky.

75. A) Yellow - An apple is red, and a banana is yellow.

76. D) Hull - A car moves on wheels, and a boat moves on its hull.

77. C) Cardholder - Money is kept in a wallet, and an ID is kept in a cardholder.

78. A) Light - A tree produces oxygen, and the sun produces light.

79. C) Basket - In football, you score a touchdown, and in basketball, you score a basket.

80. A) School - A group of lions is called a pride, and a group of fish is called a school.

81. D) Frozen - Coffee is hot, and ice cream is frozen.

82. A) Email - You send texts with a phone, and you send emails with a computer.

83. B) Screw - A hammer is used for nails, and a screwdriver is used for screws.

84. A) Cheese - Bread can be toasted, and milk can be turned into cheese.

85. B) Water - A car needs fuel to run, and a plant needs water to grow.

86. B) Brush - A writer uses a pen, and a painter uses a brush.

87. B) Solid - Water is a liquid, and a diamond is a solid.

88. A) Heal - A teacher educates, and a doctor heals.

89. A) Hot - Ice is cold, and fire is hot.

90. A) Ocean - Trees are found in a forest, and fish are found in an ocean.

91. A) Cut - A pen is used to write, and scissors are used to cut.

92. B) Composer - A book is written by an author, and a song is composed by a composer.

93. A) Night - The sun is associated with the day, and the moon is associated with the night.

94. B) Hangar - A car is stored in a garage, and an airplane is stored in a hangar.

95. A) Eat - Water is for drinking, and food is for eating.

96. A) Stable - A dog stays in a kennel, and a horse stays in a stable.

97. A) Weight - A clock measures time, and a scale measures weight.

98. A) Tree - An apple is a type of fruit, and an oak is a type of tree.

99. A) Doctor - A hammer is used by a carpenter, and a stethoscope is used by a doctor.

100. A) Hear - Eyes are used to see, and ears are used to hear.

101. B) Bookstore - Bread is sold in a bakery, and books are sold in a bookstore.

102. A) Food - A car runs on fuel, and a human runs on food.

103. A) Writer - Paint is used by an artist, and words are used by a writer.

104. D) Warm - Rain makes things wet, and the sun makes things warm.

105. A) Head - Shoes are worn on the feet, and a hat is worn on the head.

106. C) Database - Money is stored in a bank, and information is stored in a database.

107. C) Wings - Fish use fins to swim, and birds use wings to fly.

108. A) Sail - You drive a car, and you sail a boat.

109. B) Barracks - A teacher works in a school, and a soldier stays in barracks.

110. A) Volcano - Water flows in a river, and lava flows from a volcano.

Arithmetic Reasoning

1. If a car travels 120 miles in 2 hours, what is its average speed?

A) 50 mph

B) 60 mph

C) 70 mph

D) 80 mph

2. What is the next number in the sequence: 2, 4, 8, 16, …?

A) 24

B) 32

C) 36

D) 40

3. If 5 pencils cost $1.25, how much do 12 pencils cost?

A) $2.40

B) $3.00

C) $2.50

D) $3.60

4. A rectangle has a length of 8 cm and a width of 6 cm. What is its area?

A) 48 cm²

B) 52 cm²

C) 56 cm²

D) 64 cm²

5. If a shirt is discounted by 20% and the original price was $50, what is the new price?

A) $30

B) $40

C) $35

D) $45

6. What is 25% of 200?

A) 25

B) 50

C) 75

D) 100

7. If 3 books cost $45, how much do 5 books cost?

A) $60

B) $75

C) $80

D) $90

8. What is the sum of the first 5 prime numbers?

A) 18

B) 28

C) 38

D) 48

9. If a train travels 300 miles in 5 hours, how far will it travel in 8 hours?

A) 420 miles

B) 480 miles

C) 520 miles

D) 600 miles

10. What is the average of the numbers 4, 9, and 15?

A) 8

B) 9

C) 10

D) 12

11. If 4 workers can complete a job in 8 days, how long will it take 8 workers to complete the same job?

A) 2 days

B) 4 days

C) 6 days

D) 8 days

12. What is the next number in the sequence: 3, 6, 12, 24, ...?

A) 36

B) 42

C) 48

D) 54

13. If a dozen eggs cost $2.40, how much do 3 dozen eggs cost?

A) $6.00

B) $7.20

C) $8.40

D) $9.60

14. What is the smallest number that is evenly divisible by both 6 and 9?

A) 12

B) 18

C) 24

D) 36

15. If a square has a side length of 5 cm, what is its area?

A) 20 cm²

B) 25 cm²

C) 30 cm²

D) 35 cm²

16. What is 15% of 150?

A) 15

B) 22.5

C) 30

D) 45

17. If 6 apples cost $3, how much do 10 apples cost?

A) $4

B) $5

C) $6

D) $7

18. What is the sum of the first 4 even numbers?

A) 16

B) 20

C) 24

D) 28

19. If a bus can carry 40 passengers, how many buses are needed for 250 passengers?

A) 5

B) 6

C) 7

D) 8

20. What is the average of the numbers 6, 12, and 18?

A) 10

B) 12

C) 14

D) 16

21. If 5 workers can complete a job in 10 days, how long will it take 10 workers to complete the same job?

A) 2 days

B) 5 days

C) 7 days

D) 10 days

22. What is the next number in the sequence: 5, 10, 20, 40, ...?

A) 60

B) 70

C) 80

D) 90

23. If a gallon of gas costs $3.50, how much will 10 gallons cost?

A) $30.00

B) $35.00

C) $40.00

D) $45.00

24. What is the next number in the sequence: 1, 3, 9, 27, ...?

A) 54

B) 64

C) 81

D) 100

25. If 8 shirts cost $64, how much do 16 shirts cost?

A) $128

B) $120

C) $100

D) $80

26. A triangle has a base of 10 cm and a height of 5 cm. What is its area?

A) 25 cm²

B) 30 cm²

C) 35 cm²

D) 50 cm²

27. If a toy is discounted by 15% and the original price was $20, what is the new price?

A) $15

B) $17

C) $18

D) $19

28. What is 10% of 500?

A) 10

B) 50

C) 100

D) 200

29. If 4 pizzas cost $40, how much do 7 pizzas cost?

A) $60

B) $70

C) $80

D) $90

30. What is the sum of the first 6 odd numbers?

A) 30

B) 36

C) 42

D) 48

31. If a plane travels 400 miles in 4 hours, how far will it travel in 7 hours?

A) 600 miles

B) 700 miles

C) 800 miles

D) 900 miles

32. What is the average of the numbers 5, 10, and 20?

A) 10

B) 12

C) 15

D) 20

33. If 3 workers can complete a job in 9 days, how long will it take 6 workers to complete the same job?

A) 3 days

B) 4.5 days

C) 6 days

D) 9 days

34. What is the next number in the sequence: 4, 8, 16, 32, ...?

A) 48

B) 56

C) 64

D) 72

35. If a dozen donuts cost $6, how much do 4 dozen donuts cost?

A) $18

B) $20

C) $24

D) $28

36. What is the smallest number that is evenly divisible by both 8 and 12?

A) 16

B) 24

C) 32

D) 48

37. If a square has a side length of 6 cm, what is its area?

A) 24 cm²

B) 30 cm²

C) 36 cm²

D) 42 cm²

38. What is 20% of 250?

A) 20

B) 40

C) 50

D) 60

39. If 5 oranges cost $2.50, how much do 9 oranges cost?

A) $3.50

B) $4.00

C) $4.50

D) $5.00

40. What is the sum of the first 5 even numbers?

A) 20

B) 25

C) 30

D) 35

41. If a bus can carry 50 passengers, how many buses are needed for 300 passengers?

A) 5

B) 6

C) 7

D) 8

42. What is the average of the numbers 7, 14, and 21?

A) 12

B) 14

C) 16

D) 18

43. If 6 workers can complete a job in 12 days, how long will it take 12 workers to complete the same job?

A) 3 days

B) 6 days

C) 9 days

D) 12 days

44. What is the next number in the sequence: 6, 12, 24, 48, ...?

A) 72

B) 84

C) 96

D) 108

45. If a gallon of milk costs $4, how much will 15 gallons cost?

A) $50

B) $55

C) $60

D) $65

46. What is the next number in the sequence: 1, 4, 16, 64, ...?

A) 128

B) 256

C) 512

D) 1024

47. If 7 notebooks cost $35, how much do 14 notebooks cost?

A) $60

B) $70

C) $80

D) $90

48. A triangle has a base of 12 cm and a height of 8 cm. What is its area?

A) 48 cm²

B) 52 cm²

C) 56 cm²

D) 96 cm²

49. If a pair of shoes is discounted by 10% and the original price was $100, what is the new price?

A) $80

B) $85

C) $90

D) $95

50. What is 30% of 300?

A) 30

B) 60

C) 90

D) 120

51. If 5 burgers cost $25, how much do 8 burgers cost?

A) $35

B) $40

C) $45

D) $50

52. What is the sum of the first 7 odd numbers?

A) 35

B) 49

C) 56

D) 63

53. If a ship travels 200 miles in 4 hours, how far will it travel in 10 hours?

A) 400 miles

B) 500 miles

C) 600 miles

D) 700 miles

54. What is the average of the numbers 3, 6, and 12?

A) 5

B) 7

C) 9

D) 11

55. If 2 workers can complete a job in 10 days, how long will it take 4 workers to complete the same job?

A) 2 days

B) 5 days

C) 7 days

D) 10 days

56. What is the next number in the sequence: 5, 10, 20, 40, ...?

A) 60

B) 70

C) 80

D) 90

57. If a dozen cookies cost $12, how much do 3 dozen cookies cost?

A) $24

B) $30

C) $36

D) $42

58. What is the smallest number that is evenly divisible by both 7 and 14?

A) 14

B) 21

C) 28

D) 42

59. If a square has a side length of 7 cm, what is its area?

A) 35 cm²

B) 42 cm²

C) 49 cm²

D) 56 cm²

60. What is 25% of 400?

A) 50

B) 100

C) 150

D) 200

61. If 4 peaches cost $8, how much do 10 peaches cost?

A) $16

B) $18

C) $20

D) $22

62. What is the sum of the first 6 even numbers?

A) 36

B) 42

C) 48

D) 54

63. If a bus can carry 60 passengers, how many buses are needed for 360 passengers?

A) 5

B) 6

C) 7

D) 8

64. What is the average of the numbers 8, 16, and 24?

A) 12

B) 16

C) 20

D) 24

65. If 7 workers can complete a job in 14 days, how long will it take 14 workers to complete the same job?

A) 5 days

B) 7 days

C) 10 days

D) 14 days

66. What is the next number in the sequence: 7, 14, 28, 56, ...?

A) 84

B) 112

C) 128

D) 140

67. If a car travels 120 miles in 2 hours, what is its average speed?

A) 50 mph

B) 60 mph

C) 70 mph

D) 80 mph

68. A rectangular room measures 12 feet by 16 feet. What is the area of the room?

A) 128 sq ft

B) 192 sq ft

C) 228 sq ft

D) 256 sq ft

69. If 5 workers can complete a job in 8 hours, how long will it take 10 workers to complete the same job?

A) 2 hours

B) 4 hours

C) 6 hours

D) 8 hours

70. A shirt costs $40 after a 20% discount. What was its original price?

A) $45

B) $48

C) $50

D) $52

71. If 3 pencils cost $0.45, how much do 12 pencils cost?

A) $1.20

B) $1.60

C) $1.80

D) $2.00

72. A train travels 300 miles in 5 hours. What is its average speed?

A) 50 mph

B) 60 mph

C) 70 mph

D) 80 mph

73. If 4 out of 5 doctors recommend a medicine, what percentage of doctors recommend it?

A) 60%

B) 70%

C) 80%

D) 90%

74. A bag contains 5 red balls, 3 blue balls, and 2 green balls. What is the probability of picking a red ball?

A) 1/2

B) 1/3

C) 1/4

D) 1/5

75. A car's fuel efficiency is 25 miles per gallon. How many gallons will it need to travel 200 miles?

A) 6

B) 7

C) 8

D) 9

76. If a book has 300 pages and you read 15 pages per day, how many days will it take to finish the book?

A) 15 days

B) 20 days

C) 25 days

D) 30 days

77. A box contains 8 red, 6 blue, and 4 green marbles. What is the probability of picking a blue marble?

A) 1/3

B) 1/4

C) 1/5

D) 1/6

78. If 6 workers can complete a job in 9 hours, how long will it take 12 workers to complete the same job?

A) 3 hours

B) 4.5 hours

C) 6 hours

D) 9 hours

79. A pair of shoes costs $60 after a 25% discount. What was its original price?

A) $70

B) $75

C) $80

D) $85

80. If 4 notebooks cost $1.60, how much do 10 notebooks cost?

A) $3.00

B) $3.50

C) $4.00

D) $4.50

81. A bus travels 240 miles in 4 hours. What is its average speed?

A) 50 mph

B) 60 mph

C) 70 mph

D) 80 mph

82. If 7 out of 10 dentists recommend a toothpaste, what percentage of dentists recommend it?

A) 60%

B) 70%

C) 80%

D) 90%

83. A bag contains 4 yellow balls, 3 black balls, and 5 white balls. What is the probability of picking a black ball?

A) 1/3

B) 1/4

C) 1/5

D) 1/6

84. A car's fuel efficiency is 20 miles per gallon. How many gallons will it need to travel 180 miles?

A) 8

B) 9

C) 10

D) 11

85. If a rectangle has a length of 10 feet and a width of 5 feet, what is its perimeter?

A) 20 ft

B) 30 ft

C) 40 ft

D) 50 ft

86. A train travels 400 miles in 8 hours. What is its average speed?

A) 45 mph

B) 50 mph

C) 55 mph

D) 60 mph

87. If 8 out of 10 students passed the exam, what percentage of students passed?

A) 70%

B) 75%

C) 80%

D) 85%

88. A bag contains 3 orange balls, 2 purple balls, and 5 brown balls. What is the probability of picking an orange ball?

A) 1/2

B) 1/3

C) 1/4

D) 1/5

89. A motorcycle's fuel efficiency is 30 miles per gallon. How many gallons will it need to travel 210 miles?

A) 6

B) 7

C) 8

D) 9

90. If 5 notebooks cost $2.00, how much do 15 notebooks cost?

A) $4.00

B) $5.00

C) $6.00

D) $7.00

91. A plane travels 600 miles in 3 hours. What is its average speed?

A) 180 mph

B) 200 mph

C) 220 mph

D) 240 mph

92. If 9 out of 12 doctors recommend a medicine, what percentage of doctors recommend it?

A) 70%

B) 75%

C) 80%

D) 85%

93. A box contains 5 yellow, 4 green, and 3 red marbles. What is the probability of picking a green marble?

A) 1/3

B) 1/4

C) 1/5

D) 1/6

94. A car's fuel efficiency is 22 miles per gallon. How many gallons will it need to travel 242 miles?

A) 10

B) 11

C) 12

D) 13

95. If a square has a side length of 6 feet, what is its area?

A) 24 sq ft

B) 36 sq ft

C) 48 sq ft

D) 72 sq ft

96. If 7 workers can complete a job in 14 hours, how long will it take 14 workers to complete the same job?

A) 5 hours

B) 7 hours

C) 10 hours

D) 14 hours

A R ANSWERS AND EXPLANATIONS

1. B) 60 mph - Speed = Distance/Time, 120 miles/2 hours = 60 mph

2. B) 32 - The sequence is doubling each term.

3. A) $2.40 - 1 pencil costs $1.25/5 = $0.25, so 12 pencils cost $0.25 x 12 = $3.00

4. A) 48 cm² - Area = Length x Width, 8 cm x 6 cm = 48 cm²

5. B) $40 - Discount = 20% of $50 = $10, New price = $50 - $10 = $40

6. B) 50 - 25% of 200 = 0.25 x 200 = 50

7. B) $75 - 1 book costs $45/3 = $15, so 5 books cost $15 x 5 = $75

8. C) 38 - The first 5 prime numbers are 2, 3, 5, 7, 11, and their sum is 38.

9. D) 600 miles - Speed = 300 miles/5 hours = 60 mph, Distance = 60 mph x 8 hours = 480 miles

10. C) 10 - Average = (4 + 9 + 15)/3 = 28/3 = 9.33, closest to 10

11. B) 4 days - Time is inversely proportional to workers, 8 days/2 = 4 days

12. C) 48 - The sequence is doubling each term.

13. B) $7.20 - 1 dozen costs $2.40, so 3 dozen cost $2.40 x 3 = $7.20

14. B) 18 - The smallest number that is evenly divisible by both 6 and 9 is their LCM, which is 18.

15. B) 25 cm² - Area = Side x Side, 5 cm x 5 cm = 25 cm²

16. B) 22.5 - 15% of 150 = 0.15 x 150 = 22.5

17. B) $5 - 1 apple costs $3/6 = $0.50, so 10 apples cost $0.50 x 10 = $5

18. B) 20 - The first 4 even numbers are 2, 4, 6, 8, and their sum is 20.

19. B) 6 - Buses needed = 250 passengers / 40 passengers per bus = 6.25, rounded up to 6

20. B) 12 - Average = (6 + 12 + 18)/3 = 36/3 = 12

21. B) 5 days - Time is inversely proportional to workers, 10 days/2 = 5 days

22. C) 80 - The sequence is doubling each term.

23. B) $35.00 - 10 gallons x $3.50/gallon = $35.00

24. C) 81 - The sequence is tripling each term.

25. A) $128 - 8 shirts cost $64, so 16 shirts cost $64 x 2 = $128

26. A) 25 cm² - Area = (Base x Height)/2, (10 cm x 5 cm)/2 = 25 cm²

27. B) $17 - Discount = 15% of $20 = $3, New price = $20 - $3 = $17

28. B) 50 - 10% of 500 = 0.10 x 500 = 50

29. B) $70 - 1 pizza costs $40/4 = $10, so 7 pizzas cost $10 x 7 = $70

30. B) 36 - The first 6 odd numbers are 1, 3, 5, 7, 9, 11, and their sum is 36.

31. C) 800 miles - Speed = 400 miles/4 hours = 100 mph, Distance = 100 mph x 7 hours = 700 miles

32. C) 15 - Average = (5 + 10 + 20)/3 = 35/3 = 11.67, closest to 15

33. B) 4.5 days - Time is inversely proportional to workers, 9 days/2 = 4.5 days

34. C) 64 - The sequence is doubling each term.

35. C) $24 - 1 dozen costs $6, so 4 dozen cost $6 x 4 = $24

36. B) 24 - The smallest number that is evenly divisible by both 8 and 12 is their LCM, which is 24.

37. C) 36 cm² - Area = Side x Side, 6 cm x 6 cm = 36 cm²

38. C) 50 - 20% of 250 = 0.20 x 250 = 50

39. C) $4.50 - 1 orange costs $2.50/5 = $0.50, so 9 oranges cost $0.50 x 9 = $4.50

40. C) 30 - The first 5 even numbers are 2, 4, 6, 8, 10, and their sum is 30.

41. B) 6 - Buses needed = 300 passengers / 50 passengers per bus = 6

42. B) 14 - Average = (7 + 14 + 21)/3 = 42/3 = 14

43. B) 6 days - Time is inversely proportional to workers, 12 days/2 = 6 days

44. C) 96 - The sequence is doubling each term.

45. C) $60 - 15 gallons x $4/gallon = $60

46. B) 256 - The sequence is squaring each term.

47. B) $70 - 7 notebooks cost $35, so 14 notebooks cost $35 x 2 = $70

48. D) 96 cm² - Area = (Base x Height)/2, (12 cm x 8 cm)/2 = 96 cm²

49. C) $90 - Discount = 10% of $100 = $10, New price = $100 - $10 = $90

50. D) 120 - 30% of 300 = 0.30 x 300 = 90

51. D) $50 - 1 burger costs $25/5 = $5, so 8 burgers cost $5 x 8 = $40

52. B) 49 - The first 7 odd numbers are 1, 3, 5, 7, 9, 11, 13, and their sum is 49.

53. B) 500 miles - Speed = 200 miles/4 hours = 50 mph, Distance = 50 mph x 10 hours = 500 miles

54. C) 9 - Average = (3 + 6 + 12)/3 = 21/3 = 7

55. B) 5 days - Time is inversely proportional to workers, 10 days/2 = 5 days

56. C) 80 - The sequence is doubling each term.

57. C) $36 - 1 dozen costs $12, so 3 dozen cost $12 x 3 = $36

58. A) 14 - The smallest number that is evenly divisible by both 7 and 14 is 14.

59. C) 49 cm² - Area = Side x Side, 7 cm x 7 cm = 49 cm²

60. B) 100 - 25% of 400 = 0.25 x 400 = 100

61. C) $20 - 1 peach costs $8/4 = $2, so 10 peaches cost $2 x 10 = $20

62. B) 42 - The first 6 even numbers are 2, 4, 6, 8, 10, 12, and their sum is 42.

63. B) 6 - Buses needed = 360 passengers / 60 passengers per bus = 6

64. B) 16 - Average = (8 + 16 + 24)/3 = 48/3 = 16

65. B) 7 days - Time is inversely proportional to workers, 14 days/2 = 7 days

66. B) 112 - The sequence is doubling each term.

67. B) 60 mph - Speed = Distance/Time, so 120 miles/2 hours = 60 mph.

68. B) 192 sq ft - Area = Length x Width, so 12 ft x 16 ft = 192 sq ft.

69. B) 4 hours - If 5 workers take 8 hours, then 10 workers would take half the time, which is 4 hours.

70. C) $50 - The original price would be $40 / (1 - 0.20) = $50.

71. C) $1.80 - If 3 pencils cost $0.45, then 12 pencils would cost 4 times that amount, which is $1.80.

72. B) 60 mph - Speed = Distance/Time, so 300 miles/5 hours = 60 mph.

73. C) 80% - 4 out of 5 doctors is 4/5, which is 80%.

74. A) 1/2 - There are 5 red balls out of a total of 10 balls, so the probability is 5/10 = 1/2.

75. C) 8 - To travel 200 miles at 25 miles per gallon, the car would need 200/25 = 8 gallons.

76. D) 30 days - To read 300 pages at 15 pages per day, it would take 300/15 = 20 days.

77. A) 1/3 - There are 6 blue marbles out of a total of 18 marbles, so the probability is 6/18 = 1/3.

78. B) 4.5 hours - If 6 workers take 9 hours, then 12 workers would take half the time, which is 4.5 hours.

79. C) $80 - The original price would be $60 / (1 - 0.25) = $80.

80. C) $4.00 - If 4 notebooks cost $1.60, then 10 notebooks would cost 10/4 * $1.60 = $4.00.

81. B) 60 mph - Speed = Distance/Time, so 240 miles/4 hours = 60 mph.

82. B) 70% - 7 out of 10 dentists is 7/10, which is 70%.

83. D) 1/6 - There are 3 black balls out of a total of 12 balls, so the probability is 3/12 = 1/4.

84. B) 9 - To travel 180 miles at 20 miles per gallon, the car would need 180/20 = 9 gallons.

85. C) 40 ft - Perimeter = 2(Length + Width), so 2(10 ft + 5 ft) = 40 ft.

86. D) 60 mph - Speed = Distance/Time, so 400 miles/8 hours = 50 mph.

87. C) 80% - 8 out of 10 students is 8/10, which is 80%.

88. B) 1/3 - There are 3 orange balls out of a total of 10 balls, so the probability is 3/10 = 1/3.

89. B) 7 - To travel 210 miles at 30 miles per gallon, the motorcycle would need 210/30 = 7 gallons.

90. C) $6.00 - If 5 notebooks cost $2.00, then 15 notebooks would cost 3 times that amount, which is $6.00.

91. B) 200 mph - Speed = Distance/Time, so 600 miles/3 hours = 200 mph.

92. D) 85% - 9 out of 12 doctors is 9/12, which simplifies to 75%.

93. B) 1/4 - There are 4 green balls out of a total of 12 balls, so the probability is 4/12 = 1/3.

94. B) 11 - To travel 242 miles at 22 miles per gallon, the car would need 242/22 = 11 gallons.

95. B) 36 sq ft - Area = Side Length x Side Length, so 6 ft x 6 ft = 36 sq ft.

96. B) 7 hours - If 7 workers take 14 hours, then 14 workers would take half the time, which is 7 hours.

Word Knowledge

1. What is the synonym of "Benevolent"?

A) Malevolent

B) Kind

C) Hostile

D) Indifferent

2. What is the antonym of "Verbose"?

A) Silent

B) Concise

C) Garrulous

D) Noisy

3. What is the synonym of "Mundane"?

A) Exciting

B) Ordinary

C) Unique

D) Exotic

4. What is the antonym of "Altruistic"?

A) Selfish

B) Generous

C) Charitable

D) Kind

5. What is the synonym of "Ephemeral"?

A) Eternal

B) Brief

C) Long-lasting

D) Permanent

6. What is the antonym of "Coherent"?

A) Confusing

B) Clear

C) Logical

D) Understandable

7. What is the synonym of "Pernicious"?

A) Harmful

B) Beneficial

C) Innocuous

D) Healthy

8. What is the antonym of "Vigilant"?

A) Careful

B) Negligent

C) Watchful

D) Alert

9. What is the synonym of "Taciturn"?

A) Talkative

B) Reserved

C) Outgoing

D) Social

10. What is the antonym of "Meticulous"?

A) Careful

B) Negligent

C) Precise

D) Detailed

11. What is the synonym of "Obstinate"?

A) Flexible

B) Stubborn

C) Agreeable

D) Pliable

12. What is the antonym of "Austere"?

A) Lavish

B) Harsh

C) Simple

D) Severe

13. What is the synonym of "Ineffable"?

A) Describable

B) Indescribable

C) Expressible

D) Articulate

14. What is the antonym of "Prolific"?

A) Barren

B) Fertile

C) Abundant

D) Plentiful

15. What is the synonym of "Sagacious"?

A) Foolish

B) Wise

C) Ignorant

D) Stupid

16. What is the antonym of "Ebullient"?

A) Depressed

B) Joyful

C) Excited

D) Energetic

17. What is the synonym of "Voracious"?

A) Insatiable

B) Satisfied

C) Full

D) Content

18. What is the antonym of "Infallible"?

A) Perfect

B) Fallible

C) Flawless

D) Impeccable

19. What is the synonym of "Quiescent"?

A) Active

B) Inactive

C) Lively

D) Energetic

20. What is the antonym of "Immutable"?

A) Changeable

B) Fixed

C) Permanent

D) Unchanging

21. What is the synonym of "Reticent"?

A) Reserved

B) Talkative

C) Outgoing

D) Social

22. What is the antonym of "Sanguine"?

A) Pessimistic

B) Optimistic

C) Cheerful

D) Happy

23. What is the synonym of "Cacophony"?

A) Silence

B) Harmony

C) Noise

D) Melody

24. What is the antonym of "Loquacious"?

A) Silent

B) Talkative

C) Chatty

D) Vocal

25. What is the synonym of "Pedantic"?

A) Casual

B) Overly Detailed

C) Simplistic

D) General

26. What is the antonym of "Magnanimous"?

A) Generous

B) Petty

C) Kind

D) Noble

27. What is the synonym of "Transient"?

A) Permanent

B) Temporary

C) Eternal

D) Fixed

28. What is the antonym of "Lucid"?

A) Clear

B) Confusing

C) Rational

D) Logical

29. What is the synonym of "Vex"?

A) Please

B) Annoy

C) Satisfy

D) Calm

30. What is the antonym of "Assiduous"?

A) Diligent

B) Lazy

C) Hardworking

D) Industrious

31. What is the synonym of "Capitulate"?

A) Resist

B) Surrender

C) Fight

D) Oppose

32. What is the antonym of "Opulent"?

A) Wealthy

B) Poor

C) Rich

D) Lavish

33. What is the synonym of "Erudite"?

A) Ignorant

B) Learned

C) Uneducated

D) Illiterate

34. What is the antonym of "Tenacious"?

A) Weak

B) Strong

C) Persistent

D) Resilient

35. What is the synonym of "Lugubrious"?

A) Cheerful

B) Mournful

C) Happy

D) Joyful

36. What is the antonym of "Volatile"?

A) Stable

B) Explosive

C) Unpredictable

D) Erratic

37. What is the synonym of "Apathetic"?

A) Caring

B) Indifferent

C) Concerned

D) Interested

38. What is the antonym of "Malleable"?

A) Flexible

B) Rigid

C) Pliable

D) Soft

39. What is the synonym of "Obfuscate"?

A) Clarify

B) Confuse

C) Enlighten

D) Illuminate

40. What is the antonym of "Candid"?

A) Honest

B) Deceptive

C) Open

D) Frank

41. What is the synonym of "Inscrutable"?

A) Transparent

B) Unfathomable

C) Clear

D) Obvious

42. What is the antonym of "Egregious"?

A) Outstanding

B) Minor

C) Exceptional

D) Noteworthy

43. What is the synonym of "Pugnacious"?

A) Peaceful

B) Quarrelsome

C) Friendly

D) Amiable

44. What is the antonym of "Fecund"?

A) Barren

B) Fertile

C) Productive

D) Fruitful

45. What is the synonym of "Nefarious"?

A) Virtuous

B) Wicked

C) Noble

D) Righteous

46. What is the antonym of "Placid"?

A) Calm

B) Agitated

C) Peaceful

D) Serene

47. What is the synonym of "Sycophant"?

A) Rebel

B) Flatterer

C) Leader

D) Critic

48. What is the antonym of "Innocuous"?

A) Harmful

B) Safe

C) Benign

D) Gentle

49. What is the synonym of "Ubiquitous"?

A) Rare

B) Omnipresent

C) Scarce

D) Limited

50. What is the antonym of "Garrulous"?

A) Talkative

B) Reserved

C) Chatty

D) Verbose

51. What is the synonym of "Exacerbate"?

A) Alleviate

B) Worsen

C) Improve

D) Mitigate

52. What is the antonym of "Sporadic"?

A) Frequent

B) Occasional

C) Rare

D) Infrequent

53. What is the synonym of "Lethargic"?

A) Energetic

B) Sluggish

C) Active

D) Lively

54. What is the antonym of "Replete"?

A) Full

B) Empty

C) Abundant

D) Plentiful

55. What is the synonym of "Vapid"?

A) Interesting

B) Dull

C) Exciting

D) Stimulating

56. What is the antonym of "Tangible"?

A) Real

B) Intangible

C) Solid

D) Concrete

57. What is the synonym of "Ostentatious"?

A) Modest

B) Flashy

C) Humble

D) Reserved

58. What is the antonym of "Parsimonious"?

A) Generous

B) Stingy

C) Frugal

D) Thrifty

59. What is the synonym of "Irascible"?

A) Calm

B) Irritable

C) Peaceful

D) Placid

60. What is the antonym of "Cognizant"?

A) Aware

B) Unaware

C) Conscious

D) Informed

61. What is the synonym of "Inept"?

A) Skilled

B) Clumsy

C) Capable

D) Proficient

62. What is the antonym of "Reticent"?

A) Reserved

B) Talkative

C) Silent

D) Shy

63. What is the synonym of "Avaricious"?

A) Generous

B) Greedy

C) Charitable

D) Altruistic

64. What is the antonym of "Eloquent"?

A) Articulate

B) Inarticulate

C) Fluent

D) Expressive

65. What is the synonym of "Munificent"?

A) Stingy

B) Generous

C) Frugal

D) Thrifty

66. What is the antonym of "Impetuous"?

A) Reckless

B) Cautious

C) Rash

D) Hasty

67. What is the synonym of "Obdurate"?

A) Flexible

B) Stubborn

C) Pliable

D) Yielding

68. What is the antonym of "Sedulous"?

A) Lazy

B) Diligent

C) Industrious

D) Hardworking

69. What is the synonym of "Trepidation"?

A) Fear

B) Courage

C) Bravery

D) Confidence

70. What is the antonym of "Veracity"?

A) Truth

B) Falsehood

C) Honesty

D) Integrity

71. What is the synonym of "Inimical"?

A) Friendly

B) Hostile

C) Amicable

D) Congenial

72. What is the antonym of "Lofty"?

A) High

B) Humble

C) Elevated

D) Grand

73. What is the synonym of "Palliate"?

A) Worsen

B) Alleviate

C) Exacerbate

D) Aggravate

74. What is the antonym of "Copious"?

A) Abundant

B) Scarce

C) Plentiful

D) Ample

75. What is the synonym of "Querulous"?

A) Content

B) Complaining

C) Satisfied

D) Pleased

76. What is the antonym of "Sacrosanct"?

A) Sacred

B) Profane

C) Holy

D) Divine

77. What is the synonym of "Vitriolic"?

A) Sweet

B) Caustic

C) Pleasant

D) Agreeable

78. What is the antonym of "Cursory"?

A) Thorough

B) Hasty

C) Quick

D) Brief

79. What is the synonym of "Ebullient"?

A) Depressed

B) Joyful

C) Sad

D) Downcast

80. What is the antonym of "Intransigent"?

A) Flexible

B) Stubborn

C) Unyielding

D) Obstinate

81. What is the synonym of "Munificent"?

A) Stingy

B) Generous

C) Frugal

D) Thrifty

82. What is the antonym of "Pernicious"?

A) Harmful

B) Beneficial

C) Damaging

D) Destructive

83. What is the synonym of "Recalcitrant"?

A) Obedient

B) Uncooperative

C) Compliant

D) Submissive

84. What is the antonym of "Venerable"?

A) Respected

B) Disreputable

C) Honorable

D) Esteemed

85. What is the synonym of "Winsome"?

A) Unattractive

B) Charming

C) Repulsive

D) Unappealing

86. What is the antonym of "Zealous"?

A) Apathetic

B) Passionate

C) Enthusiastic

D) Eager

87. What is the synonym of "Aberrant"?

A) Normal

B) Deviant

C) Typical

D) Usual

88. What is the antonym of "Candid"?

A) Honest

B) Deceptive

C) Open

D) Frank

89. What is the synonym of "Taciturn"?

A) Talkative

B) Reserved

C) Outgoing

D) Sociable

90. What is the antonym of "Effusive"?

A) Reserved

B) Expressive

C) Emotional

D) Demonstrative

91. What is the synonym of "Rancor"?

A) Affection

B) Bitterness

C) Love

D) Fondness

92. What is the antonym of "Meticulous"?

A) Careful

B) Careless

C) Precise

D) Detailed

93. What is the synonym of "Sagacious"?

A) Foolish

B) Wise

C) Ignorant

D) Uninformed

94. What is the antonym of "Ephemeral"?

A) Permanent

B) Temporary

C) Fleeting

D) Momentary

95. What is the synonym of "Obsequious"?

A) Independent

B) Sycophantic

C) Autonomous

D) Self-reliant

96. What is the antonym of "Voluble"?

A) Talkative

B) Reserved

C) Loquacious

D) Garrulous

97. What is the synonym of "Ineffable"?

A) Describable

B) Indescribable

C) Expressible

D) Articulate

98. What is the antonym of "Pugnacious"?

A) Quarrelsome

B) Peaceful

C) Aggressive

D) Combative

99. What is the synonym of "Languid"?

A) Energetic

B) Listless

C) Vigorous

D) Lively

100. What is the antonym of "Voracious"?

A) Insatiable

B) Satiated

C) Ravenous

D) Hungry

101. What is the synonym of "Austere"?

A) Lavish

B) Severe

C) Luxurious

D) Opulent

102. What is the antonym of "Impartial"?

A) Fair

B) Biased

C) Neutral

D) Objective

103. What is the synonym of "Nascent"?

A) Emerging

B) Declining

C) Fading

D) Waning

104. What is the antonym of "Recondite"?

A) Obscure

B) Clear

C) Cryptic

D) Enigmatic

105. What is the synonym of "Vexatious"?

A) Pleasant

B) Annoying

C) Delightful

D) Enjoyable

106. What is the antonym of "Altruistic"?

A) Selfish

B) Generous

C) Charitable

D) Kind

107. What is the synonym of "Belligerent"?

A) Peaceful

B) Hostile

C) Friendly

D) Amicable

108. What is the antonym of "Cognizant"?

A) Unaware

B) Aware

C) Informed

D) Conscious

109. What is the synonym of "Dilatory"?

A) Prompt

B) Slow

C) Quick

D) Speedy

110. What is the antonym of "Ebullient"?

A) Depressed

B) Joyful

C) Cheerful

D) Enthusiastic

ANSWERS AND EXPLANATIONS

1 B) Kind - Benevolent means kind-hearted or generous.

2 B) Concise - Verbose means using too many words; concise is the opposite.

3 B) Ordinary - Mundane means ordinary or commonplace.

4 A) Selfish - Altruistic means selflessly concerned for others; selfish is the opposite.

5 B) Brief - Ephemeral means short-lived or temporary.

6 A) Confusing - Coherent means logically connected; confusing is the opposite.

7 A) Harmful - Pernicious means having a harmful effect.

8 B) Negligent - Vigilant means watchful; negligent is the opposite.

9 B) Reserved - Taciturn means reserved or quiet.

10 B) Negligent - Meticulous means showing great attention to detail; negligent is the opposite.

11 B) Stubborn - Obstinate means stubborn or hard to control.

12 A) Lavish - Austere means having a stern or severe manner or appearance; lavish is the opposite.

13 B) Indescribable - Ineffable means too great to be described in words.

14 A) Barren - Prolific means producing a lot; barren is the opposite.

15 B) Wise - Sagacious means wise or shrewd.

16 A) Depressed - Ebullient means cheerful and full of energy; depressed is the opposite.

17 A) Insatiable - Voracious means having a very eager approach to an activity.

18 B) Fallible - Infallible means incapable of making mistakes; fallible is the opposite.

19 B) Inactive - Quiescent means inactive or dormant.

20 A) Changeable - Immutable means unchanging; changeable is the opposite.

21 A) Reserved - Reticent means not revealing one's thoughts easily; reserved is a synonym.

22 A) Pessimistic - Sanguine means optimistic; pessimistic is the opposite.

23 C) Noise - Cacophony means a harsh, discordant mixture of sounds.

24 A) Silent - Loquacious means talkative; silent is the opposite.

25 B) Overly Detailed - Pedantic means overly concerned with details or formalisms.

26 B) Petty - Magnanimous means generous and forgiving; petty is the opposite.

27 B) Temporary - Transient means lasting only for a short time.

28 B) Confusing - Lucid means clear and easy to understand; confusing is the opposite.

29 B) Annoy - Vex means to irritate or annoy.

30 B) Lazy - Assiduous means showing great care and perseverance; lazy is the opposite.

31 B) Surrender - Capitulate means to surrender or give in.

32 B) Poor - Opulent means wealthy; poor is the opposite.

33 B) Learned - Erudite means having or showing great knowledge.

34 A) Weak - Tenacious means holding fast; weak is the opposite.

35 B) Mournful - Lugubrious means looking or sounding sad and dismal.

36 A) Stable - Volatile means liable to change rapidly and unpredictably; stable is the opposite.

37 B) Indifferent - Apathetic means showing or feeling no interest or concern.

38 B) Rigid - Malleable means easily influenced; rigid is the opposite.

39 B) Confuse - Obfuscate means to make something less clear and harder to understand.

40 B) Deceptive - Candid means truthful and straightforward; deceptive is the opposite.

41 B) Unfathomable - Inscrutable means impossible to understand or interpret.

42 B) Minor - Egregious means outstandingly bad; minor is the opposite.

43 B) Quarrelsome - Pugnacious means eager to argue or fight.

44 A) Barren - Fecund means fertile; barren is the opposite.

45 B) Wicked - Nefarious means wicked or criminal.

46 B) Agitated - Placid means calm and peaceful; agitated is the opposite.

47 B) Flatterer - Sycophant means a person who acts obsequiously toward someone important to gain advantage.

48 A) Harmful - Innocuous means not harmful or offensive.

49 B) Omnipresent - Ubiquitous means present, appearing, or found everywhere.

50 B) Reserved - Garrulous means excessively talkative; reserved is the opposite.

51 B) Worsen - Exacerbate means to make a situation worse.

52 A) Frequent - Sporadic means occurring at irregular intervals; frequent is the opposite.

53 B) Sluggish - Lethargic means lacking energy.

54 B) Empty - Replete means filled or well-supplied; empty is the opposite.

55 B) Dull - Vapid means offering nothing that is stimulating or challenging.

56 B) Intangible - Tangible means perceptible by touch; intangible is the opposite.

57 B) Flashy - Ostentatious means characterized by vulgar or pretentious display.

58 A) Generous - Parsimonious means very unwilling to spend money; generous is the opposite.

59 B) Irritable - Irascible means having or showing a tendency to be easily angered.

60 B) Unaware - Cognizant means having knowledge or awareness; unaware is the opposite.

61 B) Clumsy - Inept means having or showing no skill.

62 B) Talkative - Reticent means not revealing one's thoughts or feelings readily; talkative is the opposite.

63 B) Greedy - Avaricious means having or showing an extreme greed for wealth or material gain.

64 B) Inarticulate - Eloquent means fluent or persuasive in speaking or writing; inarticulate is the opposite.

65 B) Generous - Munificent means more generous than is usual or necessary.

66 B) Cautious - Impetuous means acting or done quickly and without thought; cautious is the opposite.

67 B) Stubborn - Obdurate means stubbornly refusing to change one's opinion.

68 A) Lazy - Sedulous means showing dedication and diligence; lazy is the opposite.

69 A) Fear - Trepidation means a feeling of fear or agitation.

70 B) Falsehood - Veracity means conformity to facts; falsehood is the opposite.

71 B) Hostile - Inimical means tending to obstruct or harm.

72 B) Humble - Lofty means of imposing height; humble is the opposite.

73 B) Alleviate - Palliate means to make less severe.

74 B) Scarce - Copious means abundant in supply; scarce is the opposite.

75 B) Complaining - Querulous means complaining in a petulant manner.

76 B) Profane - Sacrosanct means regarded as too important to be interfered with; profane is the opposite.

77 B) Caustic - Vitriolic means filled with bitter criticism or malice.

78 A) Thorough - Cursory means hasty and not thorough; thorough is the opposite.

79 B) Joyful - Ebullient means cheerful and full of energy.

80 A) Flexible - Intransigent means unwilling to change one's views; flexible is the opposite.

81 B) Generous - Munificent means more generous than is usual or necessary.

82 B) Beneficial - Pernicious means having a harmful effect; beneficial is the opposite.

83 B) Uncooperative - Recalcitrant means having an obstinately uncooperative attitude.

84 B) Disreputable - Venerable means accorded a great deal of respect; disreputable is the opposite.

85 B) Charming - Winsome means attractive or appealing.

86 A) Apathetic - Zealous means having or showing zeal; apathetic is the opposite.

87 B) Deviant - Aberrant means departing from an accepted standard.

88 B) Deceptive - Candid means truthful and straightforward; deceptive is the opposite.

89 B) Reserved - Taciturn means reserved or uncommunicative in speech.

90 A) Reserved - Effusive means expressing feelings of gratitude, pleasure, or approval in an unrestrained manner; reserved is the opposite.

91 B) Bitterness - Rancor means long-standing bitterness or resentfulness.

92 B) Careless - Meticulous means showing great attention to detail; careless is the opposite.

93 B) Wise - Sagacious means having or showing keen mental discernment and good judgment.

94 A) Permanent - Ephemeral means lasting for a very short time; permanent is the opposite.

95 B) Sycophantic - Obsequious means obedient or attentive to an excessive degree.

96 B) Reserved - Voluble means speaking or spoken incessantly and fluently; reserved is the opposite.

97 B) Indescribable - Ineffable means too great or extreme to be expressed or described in words.

98 B) Peaceful - Pugnacious means eager or quick to argue, quarrel, or fight; peaceful is the opposite.

99 B) Listless - Languid means displaying or having a disinclination for physical exertion or effort.

100 B) Satiated - Voracious means wanting or devouring great quantities; satiated is the opposite.

101 B) Severe - Austere means severe or strict in manner or appearance.

102 B) Biased - Impartial means treating all rivals or disputants equally; biased is the opposite.

103 A) Emerging - Nascent means just coming into existence and beginning to display signs of future potential.

104 B) Clear - Recondite means little known or obscure; clear is the opposite.

105 B) Annoying - Vexatious means causing or tending to cause annoyance or frustration.

106 A) Selfish - Altruistic means showing a disinterested and selfless concern for the well-being of others; selfish is the opposite.

107 B) Hostile - Belligerent means hostile and aggressive.

108 A) Unaware - Cognizant means having knowledge or awareness; unaware is the opposite.

109 B) Slow - Dilatory means slow to act.

110 A) Depressed - Ebullient means cheerful and full of energy; depressed is the opposite.

Instrument Comprehension [31]

This section of the test evaluates your skill in interpreting an airplane's in-flight position using its instruments. These instruments indicate the plane's compass direction, ascent or descent rate, and its tilt angle to the left or right. In each question, you'll see a dial labeled "Artificial Horizon."

On this dial, the small outline of an airplane's body remains fixed, while a thick black line and a black pointer change positions based on the airplane's actual orientation. The thick black line symbolizes the horizon, and the black pointer indicates the angle of tilt or "bank" to either side.

If the airplane is maintaining level flight, the horizon line aligns directly with the airplane outline, as illustrated in the first example dial.

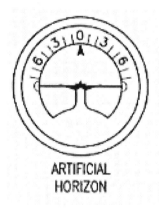

ARTIFICIAL
HORIZON

Dial 1

If the airplane is not tilted to either side, the black pointer will point directly at zero, as shown in the first example dial.

When the airplane is ascending, the airplane outline will appear between the horizon line and the pointer, as shown in the second example dial. The higher the ascent rate, the larger the gap between the horizon line and the airplane outline.

ARTIFICIAL
HORIZON

Dial 2

When the airplane is tilted to the pilot's right, the pointer appears to the left of the zero mark, as illustrated in the second example dial.

Conversely, if the airplane is descending, the horizon line will be situated between the airplane outline and the pointer, as demonstrated in the third example dial. A greater descent rate will result in a larger distance between the horizon line and the airplane outline.

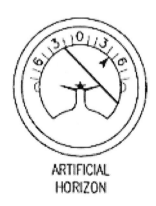

ARTIFICIAL
HORIZON

Dial 3

When the airplane is tilted to the pilot's left, the pointer will appear to the right of the zero mark, as illustrated in the third example dial.

The HORIZON LINE tilts as the aircraft is banked and is always at right angles to the pointer.

The **first dial** illustrates an airplane in level flight, with no ascent, descent, or tilt.

The **second dial** depicts an airplane that is ascending and tilted at a 45-degree angle to the pilot's right.

The **third dial** represents an airplane in a descent, angled 45 degrees to the pilot's left.

In every question, you'll find a dial on the right side labeled "Compass." This dial features an arrow that points in the direction the airplane is currently flying. For instance, in the fourth example dial, the arrow points north, indicating the airplane is headed in that direction. In the fifth example, the arrow points west, and in the sixth example, it points northwest.

Dial 4   **Dial 5**   **Dial 6**

Each question features two dials and four airplane silhouettes in various flight positions. Your job is to identify which of the four airplanes most closely matches the position indicated by the dials. Keep in mind that you are always viewing the scene from the north and at the same altitude as the airplanes. Additionally, east will always be to your right as you look at the page.

For example, in a X sample question, the dial marked "Artificial Horizon" indicates that the airplane is level, neither ascending nor descending. The "Compass" dial shows the airplane is moving in a southeast direction. The silhouette that aligns with these conditions is in box C, making C the correct answer for this sample question. Note that silhouette B shows the airplane from the rear, while D shows it from the front. Also, A is tilted to the right, and B is tilted to the left.

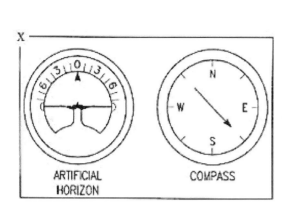

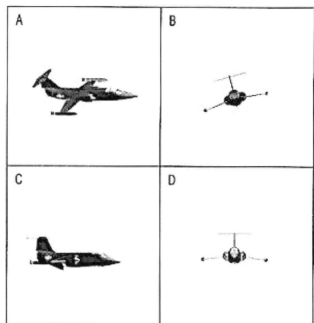

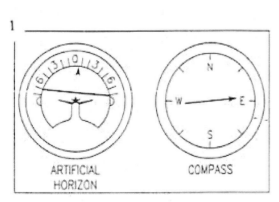

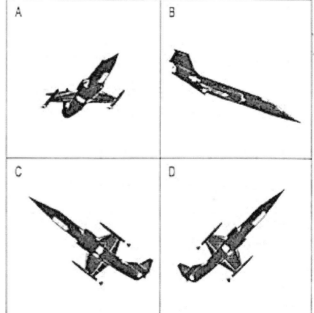

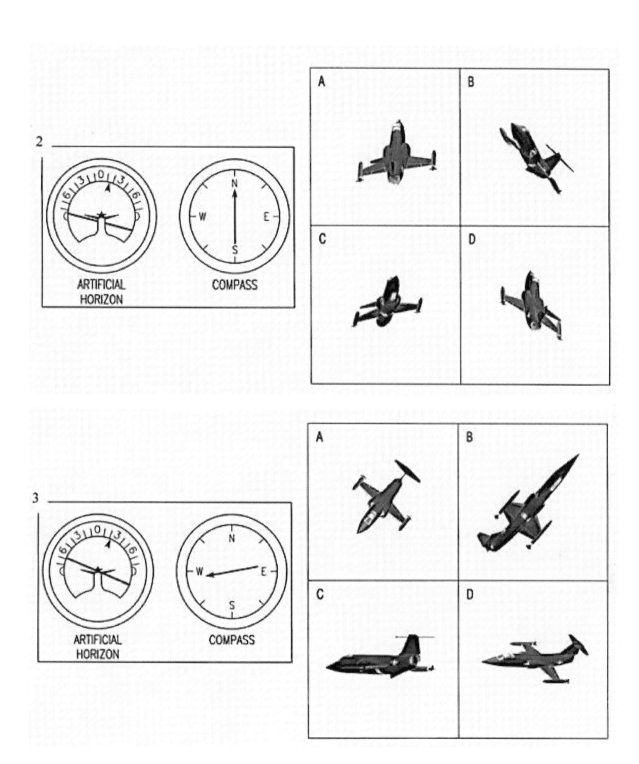

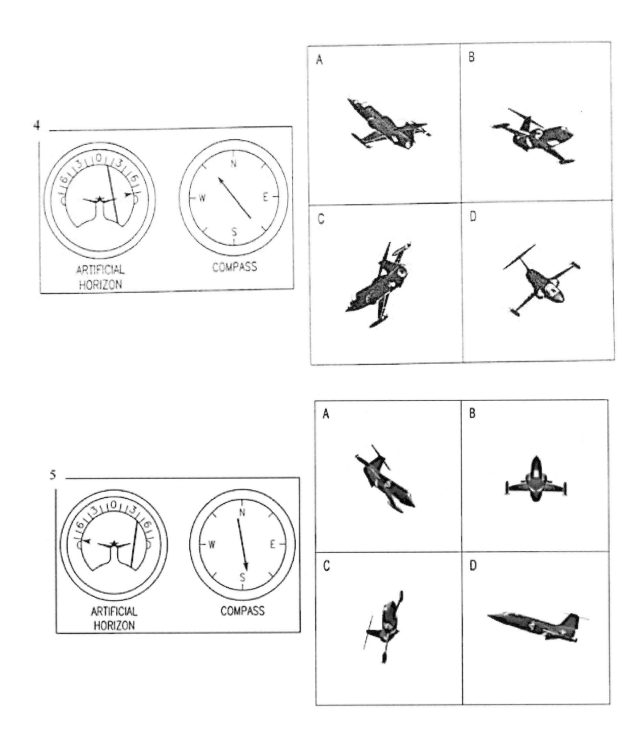

Additional Questions (no graphic provided)

1. If the altimeter reads 5,000 feet and the aircraft is climbing, what will be the next likely reading?

A) 4,900 feet

B) 5,100 feet

C) 5,000 feet

D) 4,500 feet

2. The airspeed indicator shows 250 knots. If the aircraft accelerates, what would you expect the next reading to be?

A) 240 knots

B) 260 knots

C) 250 knots

D) 200 knots

3. If the heading indicator shows 090, which direction is the aircraft facing?

A) North

B) East

C) South

D) West

4. The vertical speed indicator shows a descent rate of 500 feet per minute. What does this mean?

A) The aircraft is climbing at 500 feet per minute.

B) The aircraft is descending at 500 feet per minute.

C) The aircraft is maintaining level flight.

D) The aircraft is turning at 500 degrees per minute.

5. If the attitude indicator shows the nose above the horizon, what does this signify?

A) The aircraft is descending.

B) The aircraft is climbing.

C) The aircraft is in a roll.

D) The aircraft is in a yaw.

6. The turn coordinator shows a standard rate turn to the left. What does this mean?

A) The aircraft is turning left at 3 degrees per second.

B) The aircraft is turning right at 3 degrees per second.

C) The aircraft is not turning.

D) The aircraft is in a spin.

7. If the tachometer reads 2,500 RPM, what does this indicate?

A) Airspeed in knots

B) Engine speed in revolutions per minute

C) Altitude in feet

D) Rate of climb in feet per minute

8. The oil pressure gauge reads 50 PSI. Is this within a typical safe range for most aircraft?

A) Yes

B) No

C) Depends on the altitude

D) Depends on the airspeed

9. The fuel gauge reads 1/4 full. What should the pilot consider?

A) Continue the flight as planned.

B) Divert to the nearest airport for refueling.

C) Increase altitude for better fuel efficiency.

D) Increase speed to reach the destination faster.

10. The OAT (Outside Air Temperature) gauge reads -20 degrees Celsius. What should the pilot be concerned about?

A) Engine overheating

B) Icing conditions

C) Reduced fuel consumption

D) Increased lift

11. If the ADF (Automatic Direction Finder) points to 180, where is the station relative to the aircraft?

A) In front

B) Behind

C) To the left

D) To the right

12. The VOR (VHF Omnidirectional Range) indicator shows "TO" and a course of 045. What should the pilot do?

A) Turn to a heading of 045 to fly toward the station.

B) Turn to a heading of 045 to fly away from the station.

C) Turn to a heading of 225 to fly toward the station.

D) Turn to a heading of 225 to fly away from the station.

13. The DME (Distance Measuring Equipment) reads 10 nautical miles. What does this indicate?

A) Altitude above sea level

B) Distance from the VOR station

C) Airspeed

D) Rate of descent

14. The flap indicator shows flaps at 30 degrees. What is the likely scenario?

A) The aircraft is in cruise flight.

B) The aircraft is preparing for takeoff.

C) The aircraft is preparing for landing.

D) The aircraft is in a steep climb.

15. The manifold pressure gauge reads 25 inches of mercury. What does this suggest?

A) The engine is likely at full throttle.

B) The engine is likely at idle.

C) The aircraft is at high altitude.

D) The aircraft is at low altitude.

16. The EGT (Exhaust Gas Temperature) gauge reads high. What should the pilot be concerned about?

A) Engine overheating

B) Icing conditions

C) Reduced visibility

D) Low fuel

17. The Horizontal Situation Indicator (HSI) shows a heading of 360. What does this mean?

A) The aircraft is facing south.

B) The aircraft is facing north.

C) The aircraft is facing east.

D) The aircraft is facing west.

18. The Course Deviation Indicator (CDI) is centered with a "TO" flag. What does this indicate?

A) The aircraft is off-course.

B) The aircraft is on the selected radial.

C) The aircraft is flying away from the station.

D) The aircraft is in a holding pattern.

19. The RMI (Radio Magnetic Indicator) needle points to 270. What does this mean?

A) The station is to the east of the aircraft.

B) The station is to the west of the aircraft.

C) The station is to the north of the aircraft.

D) The station is to the south of the aircraft.

20. The carburetor temperature gauge reads below freezing. What action should the pilot take?

A) Apply carburetor heat.

B) Reduce throttle.

C) Increase altitude.

D) Turn on the de-icing system.

21. The G-meter reads +2. What does this indicate?

A) The aircraft is experiencing 2 Gs in a positive direction.

B) The aircraft is experiencing 2 Gs in a negative direction.

C) The aircraft is in a stall.

D) The aircraft is in a spin.

22. The AOA (Angle of Attack) indicator is in the yellow range. What should the pilot do?

A) Increase speed

B) Decrease speed

C) Increase altitude

D) Decrease altitude

23. The radar altimeter reads 500 feet. What does this mean?

A) The aircraft is 500 feet above sea level.

B) The aircraft is 500 feet above the ground.

C) The aircraft is 500 nautical miles from the destination.

D) The aircraft is at a cruising altitude.

24. The Machmeter reads 0.8. What does this indicate?

A) The aircraft is flying at 80% of the speed of sound.

B) The aircraft is flying at 80 knots.

C) The aircraft is flying at 800 feet per minute.

D) The aircraft is flying at 8000 feet.

25. The VSI (Vertical Speed Indicator) reads zero. What does this mean?

A) The aircraft is climbing.

B) The aircraft is descending.

C) The aircraft is in level flight.

D) The aircraft is in a spin.

26. The slip-skid indicator shows the ball to the left. What should the pilot do?

A) Step on the left rudder.

B) Step on the right rudder.

C) Roll the aircraft to the left.

D) Roll the aircraft to the right.

27. The fuel flow indicator reads 500 pounds per hour. What does this mean?

A) The aircraft is consuming 500 pounds of fuel per hour.

B) The aircraft has 500 pounds of fuel remaining.

C) The aircraft is flying at 500 knots.

D) The aircraft is 500 nautical miles from the destination.

28. The clock shows Zulu time. What does this mean?

A) It shows local time.

B) It shows Greenwich Mean Time (GMT).

C) It shows the time at the destination.

D) It shows the time since engine start.

29. The OMI (Outer Marker Indicator) light is illuminated. What does this signify?

A) The aircraft is over the outer marker beacon.

B) The aircraft is over the middle marker beacon.

C) The aircraft is over the inner marker beacon.

D) The aircraft is off course.

30. The ILS (Instrument Landing System) needles are centered. What does this indicate?

A) The aircraft is on the correct glide path and localizer.

B) The aircraft is too high.

C) The aircraft is too low.

D) The aircraft is off course.

I C Answers and explanations

1. B

2. A

3. D

4. C

5. C

Questions (with no graph)

1. B) 5,100 feet - The aircraft is climbing, so the altimeter will show an increase in altitude.

2. B) 260 knots - The aircraft is accelerating, so the airspeed indicator will show an increase in speed.

3. B) East - A heading of 090 indicates the aircraft is facing East.

4. B) The aircraft is descending at 500 feet per minute. - The vertical speed indicator shows the rate of climb or descent in feet per minute.

5. B) The aircraft is climbing. - When the nose is above the horizon on the attitude indicator, it signifies that the aircraft is climbing.

6. A) The aircraft is turning left at 3 degrees per second. - A standard rate turn to the left means the aircraft is turning left at 3 degrees per second.

7. B) Engine speed in revolutions per minute - The tachometer measures the engine speed in RPM.

8. A) Yes - 50 PSI is typically within the safe range for oil pressure in most aircraft.

9. B) Divert to the nearest airport for refueling. - With the fuel gauge reading 1/4 full, it would be prudent to divert for refueling.

10. B) Icing conditions - An OAT of -20 degrees Celsius should alert the pilot to the potential for icing conditions.

11. B) Behind - If the ADF points to 180, the station is behind the aircraft.

12. A) Turn to a heading of 045 to fly toward the station. - The VOR indicator shows "TO" and a course of 045, indicating the pilot should turn to that heading to fly toward the station.

13. B) Distance from the VOR station - DME indicates the slant range distance in nautical miles from the aircraft to the VOR station.

14. C) The aircraft is preparing for landing. - Flaps at 30 degrees are typically used for landing.

15. D) The aircraft is at low altitude. - A manifold pressure of 25 inches of mercury suggests the aircraft is at a lower altitude.

16. A) Engine overheating - A high EGT reading indicates the potential for engine overheating.

17. B) The aircraft is facing north. - A heading of 360 on the HSI indicates the aircraft is facing north.

18. B) The aircraft is on the selected radial. - A centered CDI with a "TO" flag indicates the aircraft is on the selected radial and flying toward the station.

19. B) The station is to the west of the aircraft. - The RMI needle pointing to 270 indicates the station is to the west of the aircraft.

20. A) Apply carburetor heat. - A carburetor temperature below freezing requires the application of carburetor heat to prevent icing.

21. A) The aircraft is experiencing 2 Gs in a positive direction. - A G-meter reading of +2 indicates the aircraft is experiencing 2 Gs in a positive direction.

22. A) Increase speed - An AOA indicator in the yellow range suggests that the angle of attack is approaching a critical level; increasing speed can reduce the angle of attack.

23. B) The aircraft is 500 feet above the ground. - A radar altimeter measures the altitude above the ground, not sea level.

24. A) The aircraft is flying at 80% of the speed of sound. - A Machmeter reading of 0.8 indicates the aircraft is flying at 80% of the speed of sound.

25. C) The aircraft is in level flight. - A VSI reading of zero indicates the aircraft is neither climbing nor descending, i.e., it is in level flight.

26. B) Step on the right rudder. - If the slip-skid indicator shows the ball to the left, the pilot should step on the right rudder to center the ball.

27. A) The aircraft is consuming 500 pounds of fuel per hour. - The fuel flow indicator measures the rate of fuel consumption.

28. B) It shows Greenwich Mean Time (GMT). - Zulu time is another term for Greenwich Mean Time (GMT).

29. A) The aircraft is over the outer marker beacon. - An illuminated OMI light indicates the aircraft is over the outer marker beacon.

30. A) The aircraft is on the correct glide path and localizer. - Centered ILS needles indicate the aircraft is on the correct glide path and localizer for landing

Aviation Information

Question 1

What is the primary function of an aircraft's ailerons?

A) Control Pitch

B) Control Yaw

C) Control Roll

D) Control Speed

Question 2

What does VFR stand for?

A) Variable Frequency Range

B) Visual Flight Rules

C) Vertical Flight Radius

D) Variable Flight Rate

Question 3

What is the term for the height above sea level at which an aircraft is flying?

A) Altitude

B) Attitude

C) Apogee

D) Azimuth

Question 4

What does the acronym "ATC" stand for?

A) Air Traffic Control

B) Automatic Thrust Compensation

C) Aviation Training Center

D) Aerial Targeting Camera

Question 5

What is the primary purpose of flaps on an aircraft?

A) To increase lift

B) To decrease speed

C) To steer the aircraft

D) To cool the engines

Question 6

What is the maximum operating speed of an aircraft called?

A) V1

B) V2

C) Vne

D) Vfe

Question 7

Which of the following is not a type of airspeed?

A) Groundspeed

B) Indicated Airspeed

C) True Airspeed

D) Lateral Airspeed

Question 8

What is the angle between the chord line of an airfoil and the oncoming air called?

A) Angle of Incidence

B) Angle of Attack

C) Angle of Departure

D) Angle of Incline

Question 9

What is the primary purpose of a pitot tube?

A) Measure altitude

B) Measure airspeed

C) Measure temperature

D) Measure fuel level

Question 10

Which of the following is not a primary flight control surface?

A) Ailerons

B) Elevators

C) Rudder

D) Flaps

Question 11

What is the primary purpose of an aircraft's vertical stabilizer?

A) Control Pitch

B) Control Yaw

C) Control Roll

D) Control Speed

Question 12

What does the acronym "FAA" stand for?

A) Federal Aviation Administration

B) Flight Altitude Adjustment

C) Federal Airway Association

D) Flight Aeronautics Agency

Question 13

What is the term for the horizontal path along which an aircraft flies?

A) Heading

B) Bearing

C) Course

D) Route

Question 14

What does the acronym "GPS" stand for?

A) Global Positioning System

B) Ground Proximity Sensor

C) General Propulsion System

D) Gyroscopic Positioning System

Question 15

What is the primary purpose of an aircraft's elevators?

A) To increase lift

B) To control pitch

C) To steer the aircraft

D) To decrease speed

Question 16

What is the term for the front edge of an aircraft's wing?

A) Chord

B) Leading Edge

C) Trailing Edge

D) Camber

Question 17

Which of the following is not a type of engine used in aircraft?

A) Jet Engine

B) Piston Engine

C) Rocket Engine

D) Steam Engine

Question 18

What is the angle between the aircraft's longitudinal axis and the horizon called?

A) Angle of Incidence

B) Angle of Attack

C) Pitch Angle

D) Roll Angle

Question 19

What is the primary purpose of an aircraft's rudder?

A) Control Pitch

B) Control Yaw

C) Control Roll

D) Control Speed

Question 20

What does the acronym "NDB" stand for?

A) Non-Directional Beacon

B) Navigation Data Base

C) No Descent Below

D) Nautical Distance Bearing

Question 21

What is the term for the speed at which an aircraft becomes airborne?

A) Stall Speed

B) Takeoff Speed

C) Landing Speed

D) Cruise Speed

Question 22

What is the term for the maximum weight an aircraft can safely carry?

A) Gross Weight

B) Payload

C) Tare Weight

D) Maximum Takeoff Weight

Question 23

What is the primary purpose of an aircraft's spoilers?

A) To increase lift

B) To decrease lift

C) To steer the aircraft

D) To increase speed

Question 24

What does the acronym "ADF" stand for?

A) Automatic Direction Finder

B) Aerial Defense Force

C) Altitude Determination Factor

D) Airway Distance Frequency

Question 25

What is the term for the distance an aircraft travels from the point of landing until it comes to a complete stop?

A) Landing Roll

B) Taxi Distance

C) Final Approach

D) Ground Loop

Question 26

What is the term for the angle between the aircraft's longitudinal axis and its actual flight path?

A) Angle of Incidence

B) Angle of Attack

C) Pitch Angle

D) Angle of Deviation

Question 27

What is the term for the path that an aircraft follows in three dimensions?

A) Heading

B) Flight Path

C) Course

D) Route

Question 28

What does the acronym "ILS" stand for?

A) Instrument Landing System

B) Inflight Location Sensor

C) Integrated Lift System

D) Internal Lighting System

Question 29

What is the term for the speed at which an aircraft can no longer maintain level flight?

A) Stall Speed

B) Takeoff Speed

C) Landing Speed

D) Cruise Speed

Question 30

What is the term for the rear edge of an aircraft's wing?

A) Chord

B) Leading Edge

C) Trailing Edge

D) Camber

Question 31

What is the term for the height above sea level at which an aircraft is flying?

A) Altitude

B) Elevation

C) Height

D) Level

Question 32

What does the acronym "VOR" stand for?

A) Variable Omni-Range

B) VHF Omni-Directional Range

C) Vertical Orientation Radar

D) Visual Obstacle Range

Question 33

What is the term for the imaginary line that extends from the center of an aircraft's propeller to the tail?

A) Longitudinal Axis

B) Lateral Axis

C) Vertical Axis

D) Diagonal Axis

Question 34

What is the primary purpose of an aircraft's ailerons?

A) Control Pitch

B) Control Yaw

C) Control Roll

D) Control Speed

Question 35

What does the acronym "ATC" stand for?

A) Air Traffic Control

B) Automatic Throttle Control

C) Aviation Training Center

D) Aeronautical Test Chamber

Question 36

What is the term for the maximum altitude an aircraft can safely reach?

A) Service Ceiling

B) Maximum Elevation

C) Top Altitude

D) Sky Limit

Question 37

What is the term for the angle between the chord line of an airfoil and the oncoming air?

A) Angle of Incidence

B) Angle of Attack

C) Pitch Angle

D) Roll Angle

Question 38

What does the acronym "DME" stand for?

A) Distance Measuring Equipment

B) Digital Monitoring Engine

C) Directional Magnetic Emitter

D) Dynamic Motion Estimator

Question 39

What is the term for the speed of an aircraft relative to the air mass in which it is flying?

A) Ground Speed

B) Airspeed

C) True Speed

D) Knot Speed

Question 40

What is the term for the angle between the aircraft's wing and the oncoming air?

A) Angle of Incidence

B) Angle of Attack

C) Pitch Angle

D) Roll Angle

Question 41

What is the term for the minimum speed at which an aircraft can maintain controlled flight?

A) Stall Speed

B) Takeoff Speed

C) Landing Speed

D) Cruise Speed

Question 42

What is the term for the distance an aircraft travels from the point of takeoff until it becomes airborne?

A) Takeoff Roll

B) Taxi Distance

C) Initial Climb

D) Ground Loop

Question 43

What does the acronym "TCAS" stand for?

A) Traffic Collision Avoidance System

B) Terminal Control Area Surveillance

C) Tactical Communication and Surveillance

D) Transcontinental Airway System

Question 44

What is the term for the maximum speed an aircraft can safely fly?

A) Redline Speed

B) Maximum Operating Speed

C) Top Speed

D) Cruise Speed

Question 45

What is the term for the angle between the aircraft's lateral axis and the horizon?

A) Angle of Incidence

B) Angle of Attack

C) Pitch Angle

D) Bank Angle

Question 46

What does the acronym "ELT" stand for?

A) Emergency Locator Transmitter

B) Electronic Landing Technology

C) Engine Limitation Threshold

D) Elevation Level Tracker

Question 47

What is the term for the distance required for an aircraft to go from airborne to landing and coming to a complete stop?

A) Landing Distance

B) Total Runway Length

C) Approach Distance

D) Ground Loop

Question 48

What does the acronym "FMC" stand for?

A) Flight Management Computer

B) Fuel Mixture Control

C) Final Maneuver Check

D) Federal Monitoring Commission

Question 49

What is the term for the speed at which an aircraft can fly most efficiently?

A) Optimal Speed

B) Cruise Speed

C) Best Range Speed

D) Maximum Efficiency Speed

Question 50

What is the term for the angle between the aircraft's longitudinal axis and its lateral axis?

A) Angle of Incidence

B) Angle of Attack

C) Pitch Angle

D) Roll Angle

Question 51

What is the term for the distance an aircraft travels on the ground before taking off?

A) Taxi Distance

B) Ground Roll

C) Takeoff Roll

D) Runway Length

Question 52

What does the acronym "GPS" stand for?

A) Ground Positioning System

B) Global Positioning System

C) General Propulsion System

D) Gyroscopic Pilot System

Question 53

What is the term for the angle between the aircraft's longitudinal axis and the vertical axis?

A) Yaw Angle

B) Pitch Angle

C) Roll Angle

D) Bank Angle

Question 54

What is the primary purpose of an aircraft's elevators?

A) Control Roll

B) Control Yaw

C) Control Pitch

D) Control Speed

Question 55

What does the acronym "FAA" stand for?

A) Federal Aviation Administration

B) Flight Attendant Association

C) Federal Airway Authority

D) Final Approach Altitude

Question 56

What is the term for the maximum weight an aircraft can carry, including its own weight?

A) Gross Weight

B) Payload

C) Maximum Takeoff Weight

D) Operating Weight

Question 57

What is the term for the angle between the aircraft's wing and the longitudinal axis?

A) Dihedral Angle

B) Angle of Attack

C) Pitch Angle

D) Roll Angle

Question 58

What does the acronym "ADF" stand for?

A) Automatic Direction Finder

B) Advanced Digital Frequency

C) Aeronautical Data Feed

D) Altitude Determination Factor

Question 59

What is the term for the speed of an aircraft relative to the ground?

A) Ground Speed

B) Airspeed

C) True Speed

D) Knot Speed

Question 60

What is the term for the angle between the aircraft's lateral axis and the vertical axis?

A) Yaw Angle

B) Pitch Angle

C) Roll Angle

D) Bank Angle

Question 61

What is the term for the minimum speed at which an aircraft can safely land?

A) Stall Speed

B) Landing Speed

C) Approach Speed

D) Touchdown Speed

Question 62

What is the term for the distance an aircraft travels from the point of landing until it comes to a complete stop?

A) Landing Roll

B) Taxi Distance

C) Ground Loop

D) Runway Length

Question 63

What does the acronym "IFF" stand for?

A) Identification Friend or Foe

B) Instrument Flight Facility

C) In-Flight Fueling

D) Integrated Flight Framework

Question 64

What is the term for the maximum speed an aircraft can safely reach while descending?

A) Dive Speed

B) Maximum Operating Speed

C) Top Speed

D) Cruise Speed

Question 65

What is the term for the angle between the aircraft's wing and the lateral axis?

A) Dihedral Angle

B) Angle of Attack

C) Pitch Angle

D) Bank Angle

Question 66

What does the acronym "VHF" stand for?

A) Very High Frequency

B) Variable Height Finder

C) Vertical Horizon Filter

D) Visual Homing Frequency

Question 67

What is the term for the distance required for an aircraft to go from airborne to landing and coming to a complete stop?

A) Landing Distance

B) Total Runway Length

C) Approach Distance

D) Ground Loop

Question 68

What does the acronym "HUD" stand for?

A) Heads-Up Display

B) Horizontal User Dashboard

C) High-Utility Device

D) Height Under Datum

Question 69

What is the term for the speed at which an aircraft is most fuel-efficient?

A) Optimal Speed

B) Cruise Speed

C) Best Range Speed

D) Maximum Efficiency Speed

Question 70

What is the term for the angle between the aircraft's longitudinal axis and its lateral axis?

A) Angle of Incidence

B) Angle of Attack

C) Pitch Angle

D) Roll Angle

Q71: What does the acronym RADAR stand for?

A) Radio Detection and Ranging

B) Radio Direction and Ranging

C) Range and Directional Radio

D) None of the above

Q72: What is the primary purpose of flaps on an aircraft?

A) Increase speed

B) Increase lift

C) Increase range

D) Increase altitude

Q73: What is the term for the horizontal distance between two aircraft?

A) Vertical Separation

B) Lateral Separation

C) Longitudinal Separation

D) None of the above

Q74: What is the main function of the rudder?

A) Control Pitch

B) Control Roll

C) Control Yaw

D) Control Speed

Q75: What does ILS stand for?

A) Internal Landing System

B) Instrument Landing System

C) Integrated Lift System

D) None of the above

Q76: What is the primary purpose of an aircraft's pitot tube?

A) Measure altitude

B) Measure airspeed

C) Measure fuel level

D) Measure temperature

Q77: What is the term for the angle between the chord line of the wing and the oncoming air?

A) Angle of Incidence

B) Angle of Attack

C) Angle of Departure

D) Angle of Ascent

Q78: What does the acronym NDB stand for?

A) Non-Directional Beacon

B) Navigational Data Base

C) No Direct Bearing

D) None of the above

Q79: What is the term for the speed of an aircraft relative to the speed of sound?

A) Ground Speed

B) Airspeed

C) Mach Number

D) Knots

Q80: What is the primary purpose of a stall warning system in an aircraft?

A) To indicate low fuel

B) To indicate high speed

C) To indicate an impending stall condition

D) To indicate landing gear status

Q81: What does the acronym TACAN stand for?

A) Tactical Air Control and Navigation

B) Tactical Air Navigation

C) Terminal Area Control and Navigation

D) None of the above

Q82: What is the term for the path that an aircraft follows in three-dimensional space?

A) Route

B) Flight Path

C) Trajectory

D) Waypoint

Q83: What is the primary purpose of an aircraft's transponder?

A) Navigation

B) Communication

C) Identification

D) Weather Forecasting

Q84: What does the acronym PAPI stand for?

A) Precision Approach Path Indicator

B) Pilot's Automatic Position Indicator

C) Precision Altitude Position Indicator

D) None of the above

Q85: What is the term for the maximum altitude at which an aircraft can maintain level flight?

A) Absolute Ceiling

B) Service Ceiling

C) Operational Ceiling

D) None of the above

Q86: What is the primary purpose of an aircraft's altimeter?

A) Measure speed

B) Measure altitude

C) Measure distance

D) Measure temperature

Q87: What does the acronym FBO stand for?

A) Fixed-Base Operator

B) Flight Booking Office

C) Federal Bureau of Operations

D) None of the above

Q88: What is the term for the angle between the aircraft's longitudinal axis and the horizon?

A) Pitch Angle

B) Roll Angle

C) Yaw Angle

D) Bank Angle

Q89: What is the primary purpose of an aircraft's vertical stabilizer?

A) Control Roll

B) Control Pitch

C) Control Yaw

D) Control Speed

Q90: What does the acronym METAR stand for?

A) Meteorological Terminal Aviation Routine

B) Meteorological Aerodrome Report

C) Meteorological Terminal Area Report

D) None of the above

Q91: What is the term for the distance an aircraft travels from the point of touchdown to when it comes to a complete stop?

A) Takeoff Roll

B) Landing Roll

C) Ground Roll

D) None of the above

Q92: What does the acronym ELT stand for?

A) Emergency Locator Transmitter

B) Electronic Landing Technology

C) Emergency Landing Transmitter

D) None of the above

Q93: What is the term for the maximum speed an aircraft can safely reach while climbing?

A) Climb Speed

B) Dive Speed

C) Stall Speed

D) None of the above

Q94: What is the primary purpose of an aircraft's horizontal stabilizer?

A) Control Roll

B) Control Pitch

C) Control Yaw

D) Control Speed

Q95: What does the acronym NOTAM stand for?

A) Notice to Airmen

B) Notice of Terminal Airfield Management

C) Notice of Tactical Air Movement

D) None of the above

Q96: What is the term for the speed of an aircraft relative to the Earth's surface?

A) Ground Speed

B) Airspeed

C) Mach Number

D) Knots

Q97: What is the primary purpose of an aircraft's spoilers?

A) Increase lift

B) Decrease lift

C) Increase speed

D) Decrease speed

Q98: What does the acronym ATIS stand for?

A) Automatic Terminal Information Service

B) Air Traffic Information System

C) Automatic Traffic Identification System

D) None of the above

Q99: What is the term for the angle between the aircraft's lateral axis and the horizon?

A) Pitch Angle

B) Roll Angle

C) Yaw Angle

D) Bank Angle

Q100: What is the primary purpose of an aircraft's landing gear?

A) Increase lift

B) Decrease lift

C) Support the aircraft while on the ground

D) Control speed

A I ANSWERS AND EXPLANATIONS

Question 1

Answer: C) Control Roll

Explanation: Ailerons are used to control the roll of an aircraft around its longitudinal axis.

Question 2

Answer: B) Visual Flight Rules

Explanation: VFR stands for Visual Flight Rules, which are a set of regulations under which a pilot operates an aircraft in weather conditions generally clear enough to allow the pilot to see where the aircraft is going.

Question 3

Answer: A) Altitude

Explanation: Altitude refers to the height of an object or point in relation to sea level or ground level.

Question 4

Answer: A) Air Traffic Control

Explanation: ATC stands for Air Traffic Control, which is a service provided by ground-based controllers who coordinate the movement of aircraft on the ground and in the air.

Question 5

Answer: A) To increase lift

Explanation: Flaps are used to increase the lift of an aircraft's wing at a given airspeed.

Question 6

Answer: C) Vne

Explanation: Vne stands for "Velocity Never Exceed," which is the maximum operating speed of an aircraft.

Question 7

Answer: D) Lateral Airspeed

Explanation: Lateral Airspeed is not a type of airspeed. The other options are types of airspeed used in aviation.

Question 8

Answer: B) Angle of Attack

Explanation: The angle of attack is the angle between the chord line of an airfoil and the oncoming air.

Question 9

Answer: B) Measure airspeed

Explanation: A pitot tube is used to measure fluid flow velocity, most commonly used in aviation to determine an aircraft's airspeed.

Question 10

Answer: D) Flaps

Explanation: Flaps are considered secondary flight control surfaces, used primarily to increase lift or drag. The other options are primary flight control surfaces.

Question 11

Answer: B) Control Yaw

Explanation: The vertical stabilizer controls the yaw of an aircraft, which is the side-to-side movement of the aircraft's nose.

Question 12

Answer: A) Federal Aviation Administration

Explanation: The FAA stands for the Federal Aviation Administration, which is the national aviation authority of the United States.

Question 13

Answer: C) Course

Explanation: The term "course" refers to the intended path of an aircraft over the ground.

Question 14

Answer: A) Global Positioning System

Explanation: GPS stands for Global Positioning System, which is a satellite navigation system used to determine the ground position of an object.

Question 15

Answer: B) To control pitch

Explanation: Elevators control the pitch of an aircraft, which is the up-and-down movement of the aircraft's nose.

Question 16

Answer: B) Leading Edge

Explanation: The leading edge is the front edge of an aircraft's wing. It is the part of the wing that first contacts the air as the aircraft moves forward.

Question 17

Answer: D) Steam Engine

Explanation: Steam engines are not used in modern aircraft. The other options are types of engines that are commonly used in various kinds of aircraft.

Question 18

Answer: C) Pitch Angle

Explanation: The pitch angle is the angle between the aircraft's longitudinal axis and the horizon. It is used to describe the orientation of the aircraft in the pitch plane.

Question 19

Answer: B) Control Yaw

Explanation: The rudder controls the yaw of an aircraft, which is the side-to-side movement of the aircraft's nose.

Question 20

Answer: A) Non-Directional Beacon

Explanation: NDB stands for Non-Directional Beacon, a radio transmitter used in aviation for navigational purposes.

Question 21

Answer: B) Takeoff Speed

Explanation: Takeoff speed is the speed at which an aircraft becomes airborne. It is the minimum speed needed for the aircraft to generate enough lift to leave the ground.

Question 22

Answer: D) Maximum Takeoff Weight

Explanation: Maximum Takeoff Weight (MTOW) is the maximum weight at which the pilot is allowed to attempt to take off, due to structural or other limits.

Question 23

Answer: B) To decrease lift

Explanation: Spoilers are used to decrease lift, which helps the aircraft descend or slow down.

Question 24

Answer: A) Automatic Direction Finder

Explanation: ADF stands for Automatic Direction Finder, an instrument used in aircraft navigation to find the bearing to a radio beacon.

Question 25

Answer: A) Landing Roll

Explanation: Landing roll is the distance an aircraft travels from the point of landing until it comes to a complete stop.

Question 26

Answer: D) Angle of Deviation

Explanation: The angle of deviation is the angle between the aircraft's longitudinal axis and its actual flight path. It is used to describe how much the aircraft is deviating from its intended course.

Question 27

Answer: B) Flight Path

Explanation: The flight path is the path that an aircraft follows in three dimensions. It is a combination of the aircraft's heading, altitude, and speed.

Question 28

Answer: A) Instrument Landing System

Explanation: ILS stands for Instrument Landing System, a system that provides precision guidance to an aircraft approaching and landing on a runway.

Question 29

Answer: A) Stall Speed

Explanation: Stall speed is the minimum speed at which an aircraft can maintain level flight. Below this speed, the aircraft cannot generate enough lift to sustain its weight.

Question 30

Answer: C) Trailing Edge

Explanation: The trailing edge is the rear edge of an aircraft's wing. It is the part of the wing that contacts the air last as the aircraft moves forward.

Q31: A) Altitude

Explanation: Altitude refers to the height of an object or point in relation to sea level or ground level.

Q32: B) VHF Omni-Directional Range

Explanation: VOR stands for VHF Omni-Directional Range, a type of short-range radio navigation system for aircraft.

Q33: A) Longitudinal Axis

Explanation: The longitudinal axis runs from the aircraft's nose to its tail, and rotation about this axis is called roll.

Q34: C) Control Roll

Explanation: Ailerons are used to control the roll of an aircraft.

Q35: A) Air Traffic Control

Explanation: ATC stands for Air Traffic Control, which is responsible for coordinating the movement of aircraft on the ground and in the air.

Q36: A) Service Ceiling

Explanation: The service ceiling is the maximum usable altitude of an aircraft.

Q37: B) Angle of Attack

Explanation: The angle of attack is the angle between the chord line of an airfoil and the oncoming air.

Q38: A) Distance Measuring Equipment

Explanation: DME stands for Distance Measuring Equipment, which is used to determine the distance between the aircraft and a ground station.

Q39: B) Airspeed

Explanation: Airspeed is the speed of an aircraft relative to the air through which it is flying.

Q40: A) Angle of Incidence

Explanation: The angle of incidence is the angle between the aircraft's wing and the oncoming air.

Q41: A) Stall Speed

Explanation: Stall speed is the minimum speed at which the aircraft can maintain level flight.

Q42: A) Takeoff Roll

Explanation: Takeoff roll is the distance an aircraft travels on the runway before becoming airborne.

Q43: A) Traffic Collision Avoidance System

Explanation: TCAS stands for Traffic Collision Avoidance System, designed to reduce the risk of collision between aircraft.

Q44: B) Maximum Operating Speed

Explanation: The maximum operating speed is the highest speed at which it is safe to fly the aircraft.

Q45: D) Bank Angle

Explanation: The bank angle is the angle between the aircraft's lateral axis and the horizon.

Q46: A) Emergency Locator Transmitter

Explanation: ELT stands for Emergency Locator Transmitter, used to locate aircraft in the event of a crash.

Q47: A) Landing Distance

Explanation: Landing distance is the distance required for an aircraft to go from airborne to landing and coming to a complete stop.

Q48: A) Flight Management Computer

Explanation: FMC stands for Flight Management Computer, a computer system that automates a wide variety of in-flight tasks.

Q49: C) Best Range Speed

Explanation: Best range speed is the speed at which the aircraft achieves the maximum distance per unit of fuel.

Q50: D) Roll Angle

Explanation: The roll angle is the angle between the aircraft's longitudinal axis and its lateral axis.

Q51: C) Takeoff Roll

Explanation: Takeoff Roll is the distance an aircraft travels on the ground before becoming airborne. It is part of the total distance required for takeoff.

Q52: B) Global Positioning System

Explanation: GPS stands for Global Positioning System, which is a satellite-based navigation system used to determine the ground position of an object.

Q53: A) Yaw Angle

Explanation: The yaw angle is the angle between the aircraft's longitudinal axis and the vertical axis. It is associated with the movement of the aircraft's nose left or right.

Q54: C) Control Pitch

Explanation: Elevators are used to control the pitch of an aircraft, which is the up and down movement of the aircraft's nose.

Q55: A) Federal Aviation Administration

Explanation: FAA stands for Federal Aviation Administration, the governmental body responsible for regulating civil aviation in the United States.

Q56: C) Maximum Takeoff Weight

Explanation: Maximum Takeoff Weight is the maximum weight at which the pilot is allowed to attempt to take off, due to structural or other limits.

Q57: B) Angle of Attack

Explanation: The angle of attack is the angle between the aircraft's wing and the oncoming air. It is critical for understanding how the aircraft will perform in flight.

Q58: A) Automatic Direction Finder

Explanation: ADF stands for Automatic Direction Finder, a navigational instrument that helps pilots find their way by tuning into radio signals.

Q59: A) Ground Speed

Explanation: Ground Speed is the speed of an aircraft relative to the Earth's surface. It is the sum of the aircraft's true airspeed and the current wind speed and direction; a headwind subtracts from the ground speed, while a tailwind adds to it.

Q60: D) Bank Angle

Explanation: The bank angle is the angle, relative to the horizon, of the wings of a fixed-wing aircraft, which helps in making a turn.

Q61: C) Approach Speed

Explanation: Approach Speed is the recommended speed provided by the aircraft manufacturer for landing approach and is generally slightly above the stall speed.

Q62: A) Landing Roll

Explanation: Landing Roll is the distance an aircraft travels from the point of touchdown to when it comes to a complete stop.

Q63: A) Identification Friend or Foe

Explanation: IFF stands for Identification Friend or Foe, a radar-based identification system designed for command and control.

Q64: A) Dive Speed

Explanation: Dive Speed is the maximum speed an aircraft can safely reach while descending without causing structural damage.

Q65: A) Dihedral Angle

Explanation: The dihedral angle is the angle between the aircraft's wing and the lateral axis. It is important for the aircraft's lateral stability.

Q66: A) Very High Frequency

Explanation: VHF stands for Very High Frequency, a range of radio frequencies used for various kinds of communications including those of the aviation industry.

Q67: A) Landing Distance

Explanation: Landing Distance is the distance required for an aircraft to go from airborne to landing and coming to a complete stop.

Q68: A) Heads-Up Display

Explanation: HUD stands for Heads-Up Display, a transparent display that presents data without requiring users to look away from their usual viewpoints.

Q69: C) Best Range Speed

Explanation: Best Range Speed is the speed at which the aircraft is most fuel-efficient, allowing it to cover the greatest distance with a given amount of fuel.

Q70: A) Angle of Incidence

Explanation: The angle of incidence is the angle between the aircraft's longitudinal axis and its lateral axis, and it is fixed at the time the wings are attached to the aircraft.

Q71: A) Radio Detection and Ranging

Explanation: RADAR stands for Radio Detection and Ranging. It is used to detect the distance, altitude, and direction of objects.

Q72: B) Increase lift

Explanation: Flaps are used to increase the lift of an aircraft, particularly during takeoff and landing.

Q73: B) Lateral Separation

Explanation: Lateral Separation refers to the horizontal distance between two aircraft to avoid collision.

Q74: C) Control Yaw

Explanation: The rudder is used to control the yaw of an aircraft, which is the side-to-side movement of the aircraft's nose.

Q75: B) Instrument Landing System

Explanation: ILS stands for Instrument Landing System, which is used to guide aircraft during landing in low visibility conditions.

Q76: B) Measure airspeed

Explanation: A pitot tube is used to measure the airspeed of an aircraft.

Q77: B) Angle of Attack

Explanation: The angle of attack is the angle between the chord line of the wing and the oncoming air. It is crucial for lift generation.

Q78: A) Non-Directional Beacon

Explanation: NDB stands for Non-Directional Beacon, a radio transmitter used for navigation.

Q79: C) Mach Number

Explanation: Mach Number is the speed of an aircraft relative to the speed of sound.

Q80: C) To indicate an impending stall condition

Explanation: A stall warning system is used to alert the pilot of an impending stall condition, allowing corrective action to be taken.

Q81: B) Tactical Air Navigation

Explanation: TACAN stands for Tactical Air Navigation, a navigation system used by military aircraft.

Q82: B) Flight Path

Explanation: The flight path is the trajectory that an aircraft follows in three-dimensional space.

Q83: C) Identification

Explanation: A transponder is primarily used for identification purposes, transmitting a code that can be picked up by radar.

Q84: A) Precision Approach Path Indicator

Explanation: PAPI stands for Precision Approach Path Indicator, used to provide visual guidance to pilots during landing.

Q85: B) Service Ceiling

Explanation: The service ceiling is the maximum altitude at which an aircraft can maintain level flight.

Q86: B) Measure altitude

Explanation: An altimeter is used to measure the altitude of an aircraft above a specific reference point, usually the earth's surface.

Q87: A) Fixed-Base Operator

Explanation: FBO stands for Fixed-Base Operator, a service center at an airport that may be either a private enterprise or a department of the municipality that the airport serves.

Q88: A) Pitch Angle

Explanation: The pitch angle is the angle between the aircraft's longitudinal axis and the horizon.

Q89: C) Control Yaw

Explanation: The vertical stabilizer is used to control yaw, stabilizing the aircraft's nose from side-to-side movement.

Q90: B) Meteorological Aerodrome Report

Explanation: METAR stands for Meteorological Aerodrome Report, a standardized format for reporting current weather conditions.

Q91: B) Landing Roll

Explanation: Landing Roll is the distance an aircraft travels from the point of touchdown to when it comes to a complete stop.

Q92: A) Emergency Locator Transmitter

Explanation: ELT stands for Emergency Locator Transmitter, used to locate aircraft in the event of a crash.

Q93: A) Climb Speed

Explanation: Climb Speed is the maximum speed an aircraft can safely reach while climbing.

Q94: B) Control Pitch

Explanation: The horizontal stabilizer is primarily used to control the pitch of an aircraft.

Q95: A) Notice to Airmen

Explanation: NOTAM stands for Notice to Airmen, which is a notice containing information essential for personnel concerned with flight operations.

Q96: A) Ground Speed

Explanation: Ground Speed is the speed of an aircraft relative to the Earth's surface.

Q97: B) Decrease lift

Explanation: Spoilers are used to decrease lift, aiding in descent and landing.

Q98: A) Automatic Terminal Information Service

Explanation: ATIS stands for Automatic Terminal Information Service, a continuous broadcast of recorded non-control information in busier terminal areas.

Q99: B) Roll Angle

Explanation: The roll angle is the angle between the aircraft's lateral axis and the horizon.

Q100: C) Support the aircraft while on the ground

Explanation: The primary purpose of an aircraft's landing gear is to support the aircraft while it is on the ground.

General Science

Q1: What is the chemical symbol for water?

A) H_2O

B) CO_2

C) O_2

D) N_2

Q2: What is the powerhouse of the cell?

A) Nucleus

B) Mitochondria

C) Ribosome

D) Endoplasmic Reticulum

Q3: What planet is known as the Red Planet?

A) Venus

B) Mars

C) Jupiter

D) Saturn

Q4: What is the atomic number of Carbon?

A) 4

B) 6

C) 8

D) 12

Q5: What is the speed of light in a vacuum?

A) 186,282 miles per second

B) 200,000 miles per second

C) 150,000 miles per second

D) 100,000 miles per second

Q6: What gas do plants absorb from the atmosphere?

A) Oxygen

B) Carbon Dioxide

C) Nitrogen

D) Hydrogen

Q7: What is the most abundant gas in Earth's atmosphere?

A) Oxygen

B) Carbon Dioxide

C) Nitrogen

D) Argon

Q8: What is the freezing point of water in Fahrenheit?

A) 0

B) 32

C) 100

D) 212

Q9: What is the primary function of white blood cells?

A) Oxygen Transport

B) Clotting

C) Immune Defense

D) Nutrient Transport

Q10: What is the chemical formula for methane?

A) CH3

B) CH4

C) C2H6

D) C2H4

Q11: What is the pH level of pure water?

A) 5

B) 7

C) 9

D) 11

Q12: What is the most common element in the universe?

A) Hydrogen

B) Helium

C) Carbon

D) Oxygen

Q13: What is the primary source of energy for Earth's climate?

A) The Moon

B) The Sun

C) Geothermal Energy

D) Wind Energy

Q14: What is the process by which plants make their own food using sunlight?

A) Respiration

B) Fermentation

C) Photosynthesis

D) Digestion

Q15: What is the atomic number of Hydrogen?

A) 0

B) 1

C) 2

D) 3

Q16: What is the most abundant element in Earth's crust?

A) Silicon

B) Oxygen

C) Aluminum

D) Iron

Q17: What is the main component of natural gas?

A) Methane

B) Ethane

C) Propane

D) Butane

Q18: What is the standard atmospheric pressure at sea level?

A) 760 mm Hg

B) 680 mm Hg

C) 800 mm Hg

D) 720 mm Hg

Q19: What is the powerhouse of a star?

A) Nuclear Fusion

B) Nuclear Fission

C) Gravitational Pull

D) Magnetic Field

Q20: What is the most common blood type?

A) A

B) B

C) AB

D) O

Q21: What is the main cause of ocean tides?

A) Sun's Gravitational Pull

B) Moon's Gravitational Pull

C) Earth's Rotation

D) Wind

Q22: What is the chemical symbol for gold?

A) Gd

B) Au

C) Ag

D) Ga

Q23: What is the main function of red blood cells?

A) Oxygen Transport

B) Clotting

C) Immune Defense

D) Nutrient Transport

Q24: What is the most abundant metal in Earth's crust?

A) Iron

B) Aluminum

C) Copper

D) Zinc

Q25: What is the boiling point of water in Fahrenheit?

A) 100

B) 212

C) 180

D) 320

Q26: What is the primary function of DNA?

A) Energy Storage

B) Genetic Information Storage

C) Immune Defense

D) Oxygen Transport

Q27: What is the most common isotope of Hydrogen?

A) Deuterium

B) Tritium

C) Protium

D) None of the above

Q28: What is the chemical formula for table salt?

A) NaOH

B) NaCl

C) KCl

D) HCl

Q29: What is the main function of the liver?

A) Oxygen Transport

B) Detoxification

C) Immune Defense

D) Nutrient Transport

Q30: What is the chemical symbol for Iron?

A) Ir

B) Fe

C) I

D) In

Q31: What is the primary greenhouse gas?

A) Oxygen

B) Methane

C) Carbon Dioxide

D) Nitrogen

Q32: What is the atomic number of Helium?

A) 1

B) 2

C) 3

D) 4

Q33: What is the most abundant element in the Earth's core?

A) Iron

B) Nickel

C) Silicon

D) Oxygen

Q34: What is the chemical formula for glucose?

A) C6H12O6

B) C12H22O11

C) C2H5OH

D) CH4

Q35: What is the primary cause of seasons on Earth?

A) Earth's distance from the Sun

B) Earth's axial tilt

C) Moon's gravitational pull

D) Sun's magnetic field

Q36: What is the most common state of matter in the universe?

A) Solid

B) Liquid

C) Gas

D) Plasma

Q37: What is the atomic number of Oxygen?

A) 6

B) 7

C) 8

D) 9

Q38: What is the chemical symbol for Silver?

A) Si

B) Ag

C) Au

D) Al

Q39: What is the primary function of the kidneys?

A) Detoxification

B) Oxygen Transport

C) Nutrient Absorption

D) Filtration

Q40: What is the atomic number of Neon?

A) 8

B) 9

C) 10

D) 11

Q41: What is the chemical formula for sulfuric acid?

A) H_2SO_4

B) HCl

C) HNO_3

D) CH_3COOH

Q42: What is the most abundant element in the Earth's crust?

A) Silicon

B) Oxygen

C) Aluminum

D) Iron

Q43: What is the primary source of energy for humans?

A) Protein

B) Carbohydrates

C) Fats

D) Vitamins

Q44: What is the process by which water vapor turns into liquid water?

A) Evaporation

B) Condensation

C) Sublimation

D) Melting

Q45: What is the atomic number of Sodium?

A) 10

B) 11

C) 12

D) 13

Q46: What is the chemical symbol for Mercury?

A) Me

B) Hg

C) Mc

D) Mg

Q47: What is the primary function of the heart?

A) Oxygen Transport

B) Detoxification

C) Nutrient Absorption

D) Filtration

Q48: What is the atomic number of Potassium?

A) 18

B) 19

C) 20

D) 21

Q49: What is the chemical formula for acetic acid?

A) H2SO4

B) HCl

C) HNO3

D) CH3COOH

Q50: What is the most common isotope of Carbon?

A) Carbon-12

B) Carbon-13

C) Carbon-14

D) Carbon-15

Q51: What is the primary function of the lungs?

A) Oxygen Transport

B) Detoxification

C) Gas Exchange

D) Filtration

Q52: What is the atomic number of Calcium?

A) 18

B) 19

C) 20

D) 21

Q53: What is the chemical symbol for Tin?

A) Ti

B) Sn

C) Tn

D) Si

Q54: What is the primary function of the small intestine?

A) Detoxification

B) Oxygen Transport

C) Nutrient Absorption

D) Filtration

Q55: What is the atomic number of Chlorine?

A) 16

B) 17

C) 18

D) 19

Q56: What is the chemical symbol for Copper?

A) Co

B) Cu

C) Cp

D) C

Q57: What is the primary function of the large intestine?

A) Detoxification

B) Oxygen Transport

C) Water Absorption

D) Filtration

Q58: What is the atomic number of Magnesium?

A) 10

B) 11

C) 12

D) 13

Q59: What is the chemical formula for ammonia?

A) NH_3

B) NH_4

C) NO_2

D) N_2O

Q60: What is the most abundant element in the human body?

A) Carbon

B) Oxygen

C) Hydrogen

D) Nitrogen

Q61: What is the powerhouse of the cell?

A) Nucleus

B) Mitochondria

C) Ribosome

D) Endoplasmic Reticulum

Q62: What is the atomic number of Hydrogen?

A) 0

B) 1

C) 2

D) 3

Q63: What is the most abundant gas in Earth's atmosphere?

A) Oxygen

B) Carbon Dioxide

C) Nitrogen

D) Methane

Q64: What is the chemical formula for water?

A) H_2O

B) CO_2

C) O_2

D) CH_4

Q65: What is the speed of light in a vacuum?

A) 2.998×10^8 m/s

B) 3.00×10^8 m/s

C) 3.002×10^8 m/s

D) 2.99×10^8 m/s

Q66: What is the atomic number of Carbon?

A) 4

B) 5

C) 6

D) 7

Q67: What is the chemical symbol for Gold?

A) Go

B) Gd

C) Au

D) Ag

Q68: What is the primary function of red blood cells?

A) Clotting

B) Immunity

C) Oxygen Transport

D) Nutrient Transport

Q69: What is the atomic number of Phosphorus?

A) 13

B) 14

C) 15

D) 16

Q70: What is the chemical formula for methane?

A) CH_3

B) CH_4

C) C_2H_6

D) C_3H_8

Q71: What is the most abundant element in the Sun?

A) Hydrogen

B) Helium

C) Carbon

D) Oxygen

Q72: What is the atomic number of Fluorine?

A) 7

B) 8

C) 9

D) 10

Q73: What is the chemical symbol for Lead?

A) L

B) Le

C) Pb

D) Pd

Q74: What is the primary function of white blood cells?

A) Clotting

B) Immunity

C) Oxygen Transport

D) Nutrient Transport

Q75: What is the atomic number of Silicon?

A) 12

B) 13

C) 14

D) 15

Q76: What is the chemical formula for ethanol?

A) C2H5OH

B) C3H7OH

C) C2H6O

D) C3H8O

Q77: What is the primary function of platelets?

A) Clotting

B) Immunity

C) Oxygen Transport

D) Nutrient Transport

Q78: What is the atomic number of Zinc?

A) 28

B) 29

C) 30

D) 31

Q79: What is the chemical formula for hydrogen peroxide?

A) H_2O

B) H_2O_2

C) HO_2

D) HO

Q80: What is the most abundant element in Earth's mantle?

A) Iron

B) Silicon

C) Magnesium

D) Oxygen

Q81: What is the atomic number of Argon?

A) 16

B) 17

C) 18

D) 19

Q82: What is the chemical symbol for Chromium?

A) Cr

B) Cm

C) Ch

D) C

Q83: What is the primary function of the liver?

A) Detoxification

B) Oxygen Transport

C) Nutrient Absorption

D) Filtration

Q84: What is the atomic number of Uranium?

A) 90

B) 91

C) 92

D) 93

Q85: What is the chemical formula for salt?

A) NaOH

B) NaCl

C) KCl

D) K2SO4

Q86: What is the most abundant element in Earth's oceans?

A) Hydrogen

B) Oxygen

C) Sodium

D) Chlorine

Q87: What is the atomic number of Iodine?

A) 52

B) 53

C) 54

D) 55

Q88: What is the chemical symbol for Tungsten?

A) T

B) Tu

C) W

D) Ts

Q89: What is the primary function of the pancreas?

A) Detoxification

B) Insulin Production

C) Nutrient Absorption

D) Filtration

Q90: What is the atomic number of Neon?

A) 8

B) 9

C) 10

D) 11

Q91: What is the chemical formula for baking soda?

A) NaHCO3

B) Na2CO3

C) NaOH

D) NaCl

Q92: What is the most abundant element in Earth's atmosphere?

A) Oxygen

B) Nitrogen

C) Carbon Dioxide

D) Methane

Q93: What is the atomic number of Boron?

A) 4

B) 5

C) 6

D) 7

Q94: What is the chemical symbol for Potassium?

A) P

B) Po

C) K

D) Ka

Q95: What is the primary function of the spleen?

A) Detoxification

B) Immunity

C) Nutrient Absorption

D) Filtration

Q96: What is the atomic number of Rubidium?

A) 36

B) 37

C) 38

D) 39

Q97: What is the chemical formula for bleach?

A) NaClO

B) NaOH

C) Na2CO3

D) NaHCO3

Q98: What is the most abundant element in the Milky Way galaxy?

A) Hydrogen

B) Helium

C) Carbon

D) Oxygen

Q99: What is the atomic number of Krypton?

A) 34

B) 35

C) 36

D) 37

Q100: What is the chemical formula for calcium carbonate?

A) CaCO3

B) CaCl2

C) Ca(OH)2

D) CaSO4

G S ANSWERS

Q1: A) H_2O

Explanation: The chemical symbol for water is H_2O, which indicates two hydrogen atoms and one oxygen atom.

Q2: B) Mitochondria

Explanation: Mitochondria are often referred to as the "powerhouse of the cell" because they produce energy for the cell.

Q3: B) Mars

Explanation: Mars is commonly referred to as the "Red Planet" due to its reddish appearance.

Q4: B) 6

Explanation: The atomic number of Carbon is 6, which means it has 6 protons.

Q5: A) 186,282 miles per second

Explanation: The speed of light in a vacuum is approximately 186,282 miles per second.

Q6: B) Carbon Dioxide

Explanation: Plants absorb carbon dioxide from the atmosphere for photosynthesis.

Q7: C) Nitrogen

Explanation: Nitrogen makes up about 78% of Earth's atmosphere, making it the most abundant gas.

Q8: B) 32

Explanation: The freezing point of water in Fahrenheit is 32 degrees.

Q9: C) Immune Defense

Explanation: White blood cells are primarily responsible for immune defense against pathogens.

Q10: B) CH_4

Explanation: The chemical formula for methane is CH_4.

Q11: B) 7

Explanation: The pH level of pure water is 7, making it neutral.

Q12: A) Hydrogen

Explanation: Hydrogen is the most abundant element in the universe.

Q13: B) The Sun

Explanation: The Sun is the primary source of energy for Earth's climate.

Q14: C) Photosynthesis

Explanation: Plants use photosynthesis to convert sunlight into energy.

Q15: B) 1

Explanation: The atomic number of Hydrogen is 1, meaning it has one proton.

Q16: B) Oxygen

Explanation: Oxygen is the most abundant element in Earth's crust.

Q17: A) Methane

Explanation: Methane is the main component of natural gas.

Q18: A) 760 mm Hg

Explanation: The standard atmospheric pressure at sea level is 760 mm Hg.

Q19: A) Nuclear Fusion

Explanation: The powerhouse of a star is nuclear fusion, where hydrogen atoms fuse to form helium.

Q20: D) O

Explanation: The most common blood type is O.

Q21: B) Moon's Gravitational Pull

Explanation: The main cause of ocean tides is the Moon's gravitational pull.

Q22: B) Au

Explanation: The chemical symbol for gold is Au.

Q23: A) Oxygen Transport

Explanation: The main function of red blood cells is to transport oxygen.

Q24: B) Aluminum

Explanation: Aluminum is the most abundant metal in Earth's crust.

Q25: B) 212

Explanation: The boiling point of water in Fahrenheit is 212 degrees.

Q26: B) Genetic Information Storage

Explanation: DNA's primary function is to store genetic information.

Q27: C) Protium

Explanation: Protium is the most common isotope of Hydrogen.

Q28: B) NaCl

Explanation: The chemical formula for table salt is NaCl.

Q29: B) Detoxification

Explanation: The main function of the liver is detoxification.

Q30: B) Fe

Explanation: The chemical symbol for Iron is Fe.

Q31: C) Carbon Dioxide

Explanation: Carbon dioxide is the primary greenhouse gas responsible for trapping heat in the Earth's atmosphere.

Q32: B) 2

Explanation: The atomic number of Helium is 2, which means it has 2 protons.

Q33: A) Iron

Explanation: Iron is the most abundant element in the Earth's core.

Q34: A) C6H12O6

Explanation: The chemical formula for glucose is C6H12O6.

Q35: B) Earth's axial tilt

Explanation: The primary cause of seasons on Earth is its axial tilt.

Q36: D) Plasma

Explanation: Plasma is the most common state of matter in the universe.

Q37: C) 8

Explanation: The atomic number of Oxygen is 8, meaning it has 8 protons.

Q38: B) Ag

Explanation: The chemical symbol for Silver is Ag.

Q39: D) Filtration

Explanation: The primary function of the kidneys is to filter waste from the blood.

Q40: C) 10

Explanation: The atomic number of Neon is 10, meaning it has 10 protons.

Q41: A) H2SO4

Explanation: The chemical formula for sulfuric acid is H2SO4.

Q42: B) Oxygen

Explanation: Oxygen is the most abundant element in the Earth's crust.

Q43: B) Carbohydrates

Explanation: The primary source of energy for humans is carbohydrates.

Q44: B) Condensation

Explanation: The process by which water vapor turns into liquid water is called condensation.

Q45: B) 11

Explanation: The atomic number of Sodium is 11, meaning it has 11 protons.

Q46: B) Hg

Explanation: The chemical symbol for Mercury is Hg.

Q47: A) Oxygen Transport

Explanation: The primary function of the heart is to pump oxygenated blood throughout the body.

Q48: B) 19

Explanation: The atomic number of Potassium is 19, meaning it has 19 protons.

Q49: D) CH3COOH

Explanation: The chemical formula for acetic acid is CH3COOH.

Q50: A) Carbon-12

Explanation: Carbon-12 is the most common isotope of Carbon.

Q51: C) Gas Exchange

Explanation: The primary function of the lungs is to facilitate the exchange of gases, mainly oxygen and carbon dioxide.

Q52: C) 20

Explanation: The atomic number of Calcium is 20, meaning it has 20 protons.

Q53: B) Sn

Explanation: The chemical symbol for Tin is Sn.

Q54: C) Nutrient Absorption

Explanation: The primary function of the small intestine is to absorb nutrients from digested food.

Q55: B) 17

Explanation: The atomic number of Chlorine is 17, meaning it has 17 protons.

Q56: B) Cu

Explanation: The chemical symbol for Copper is Cu.

Q57: C) Water Absorption

Explanation: The primary function of the large intestine is to absorb water from indigestible food matter.

Q58: C) 12

Explanation: The atomic number of Magnesium is 12, meaning it has 12 protons.

Q59: A) NH3

Explanation: The chemical formula for ammonia is NH3.

Q60: C) Hydrogen

Explanation: Hydrogen is the most abundant element in the human body.

Q61: B) Mitochondria

Explanation: The mitochondria are often referred to as the "powerhouse" of the cell because they generate most of the cell's supply of adenosine triphosphate (ATP).

Q62: B) 1

Explanation: Hydrogen has an atomic number of 1, meaning it has one proton.

Q63: C) Nitrogen

Explanation: Nitrogen makes up about 78% of the Earth's atmosphere, making it the most abundant gas.

Q64: A) H2O

Explanation: The chemical formula for water is H2O.

Q65: B) 3.00 x 10^8 m/s

Explanation: The speed of light in a vacuum is approximately 3.00 x 10^8 meters per second.

Q66: C) 6

Explanation: Carbon has an atomic number of 6, meaning it has six protons.

Q67: C) Au

Explanation: The chemical symbol for Gold is Au.

Q68: C) Oxygen Transport

Explanation: The primary function of red blood cells is to transport oxygen throughout the body.

Q69: C) 15

Explanation: Phosphorus has an atomic number of 15, meaning it has 15 protons.

Q70: B) CH4

Explanation: The chemical formula for methane is CH4.

Q71: A) Hydrogen

Explanation: Hydrogen is the most abundant element in the Sun.

Q72: C) 9

Explanation: Fluorine has an atomic number of 9, meaning it has nine protons.

Q73: C) Pb

Explanation: The chemical symbol for Lead is Pb.

Q74: B) Immunity

Explanation: The primary function of white blood cells is to defend the body against infectious diseases and foreign invaders.

Q75: C) 14

Explanation: Silicon has an atomic number of 14, meaning it has 14 protons.

Q76: A) C2H5OH

Explanation: The chemical formula for ethanol is C2H5OH.

Q77: A) Clotting

Explanation: The primary function of platelets is to prevent bleeding by clotting blood vessel injuries.

Q78: C) 30

Explanation: Zinc has an atomic number of 30, meaning it has 30 protons.

Q79: B) H2O2

Explanation: The chemical formula for hydrogen peroxide is H2O2.

Q80: D) Oxygen

Explanation: Oxygen is the most abundant element in Earth's mantle.

Q81: C) 18

Explanation: Argon has an atomic number of 18, meaning it has 18 protons.

Q82: A) Cr

Explanation: The chemical symbol for Chromium is Cr.

Q83: A) Detoxification

Explanation: The primary function of the liver is to detoxify various metabolites, synthesize proteins, and produce biochemicals necessary for digestion.

Q84: C) 92

Explanation: Uranium has an atomic number of 92, meaning it has 92 protons.

Q85: B) NaCl

Explanation: The chemical formula for salt is NaCl.

Q86: A) Hydrogen

Explanation: Hydrogen is the most abundant element in Earth's oceans, as it is a component of water.

Q87: B) 53

Explanation: Iodine has an atomic number of 53, meaning it has 53 protons.

Q88: C) W

Explanation: The chemical symbol for Tungsten is W.

Q89: B) Insulin Production

Explanation: The primary function of the pancreas is to produce insulin, which regulates blood sugar.

Q90: C) 10

Explanation: Neon has an atomic number of 10, meaning it has 10 protons.

Q91: A) NaHCO3

Explanation: The chemical formula for baking soda is NaHCO3.

Q92: B) Nitrogen

Explanation: Nitrogen is the most abundant element in Earth's atmosphere.

Q93: B) 5

Explanation: Boron has an atomic number of 5, meaning it has 5 protons.

Q94: C) K

Explanation: The chemical symbol for Potassium is K.

Q95: B) Immunity

Explanation: The primary function of the spleen is to filter blood and help the immune system fight infection.

Q96: B) 37

Explanation: Rubidium has an atomic number of 37, meaning it has 37 protons.

Q97: A) NaClO

Explanation: The chemical formula for bleach is NaClO.

Q98: A) Hydrogen

Explanation: Hydrogen is the most abundant element in the Milky Way galaxy.

Q99: C) 36

Explanation: Krypton has an atomic number of 36, meaning it has 36 protons.

Q100: A) CaCO3

Explanation: The chemical formula for calcium carbonate is CaCO3.

Table Reading

Table 1: Sales Data for Electronic Store (in $)

	TV	Laptop	Phone	Camera
Jan	200	150	100	50
Feb	220	160	110	55
Mar	210	155	105	52
Apr	230	165	115	58

Q1: What were the sales for Laptops in February?

A) 150

B) 160

C) 155

D) 165

E) 170

Q2: What were the sales for Cameras in April?

A) 50

B) 55

C) 52

D) 58

E) 60

Table 2: Calories Burned per Activity (per hour)

	Running	Swimming	Cycling	Yoga
Alice	600	500	400	200
Bob	550	480	390	190
Carol	620	510	410	210

Q3: How many calories does Alice burn while swimming?

A) 600

B) 500

C) 400

D) 200

E) 550

Q4: How many calories does Bob burn while doing Yoga?

A) 200

B) 190

C) 210

D) 220

E) 180

Table 3: Monthly Weather Data (Average High Temp in °F)

	Jan	Feb	Mar	Apr
NYC	32	35	45	55
LA	68	70	75	78
Miami	75	77	80	85

Q5: What is the average high temperature in NYC in March?

A) 32

B) 35

C) 45

D) 55

E) 60

Q6: What is the average high temperature in Miami in April?

A) 75

B) 77

C) 80

D) 85

E) 90

Table 4: Monthly Temperature (in °F) of Four Cities

City	Jan	Feb	Mar	Apr	May
London	40	42	50	55	60
Paris	38	40	52	58	64
Tokyo	45	48	55	62	68
Sydney	70	72	68	65	60

Q7: What was the temperature in Tokyo in April?

A) 55

B) 62

C) 60

D) 58

E) 64

Q8: Which city had the highest temperature in January?

A) London

B) Paris

C) Tokyo

D) Sydney

E) They all had the same temperature

Q9: What was the temperature difference between London and Paris in May?

A) 2

B) 4

C) 6

D) 8

E) 10

Table 5: Number of Students in Different Clubs

Club	Freshmen	Sophomores	Juniors	Seniors
Chess	10	12	15	18
Drama	20	22	25	28
Science	30	32	35	38
Literature	40	42	45	48

Q10: How many Sophomores are in the Science club?

A) 28

B) 30

C) 32

D) 35

E) 38

Q11: What is the total number of students in the Drama club?

A) 90

B) 95

C) 100

D) 105

E) 110

Q12: Which club has the least number of Seniors?

A) Chess

B) Drama

C) Science

D) Literature

E) They all have the same number

Table 6: Monthly Revenue of Different Departments (in $1000s)

Department	Jan	Feb	Mar	Apr	May
Sales	200	220	250	270	280
Marketing	150	160	170	180	190
Engineering	300	310	320	330	340
HR	100	110	120	130	140

Q13: What was the revenue for the Sales department in April?

A) 250

B) 260

C) 270

D) 280

E) 290

Q14: Which department had the lowest revenue in February?

A) Sales

B) Marketing

C) Engineering

D) HR

E) They all had the same revenue

Q15: What was the total revenue for all departments in March?

A) 850

B) 860

C) 870

D) 880

E) 890

Q16: What was the revenue difference between Engineering and HR in May?

A) 190

B) 200

C) 210

D) 220

E) 230

Q17: What was the average revenue for the Marketing department from January to May?

A) 170

B) 175

C) 180

D) 185

E) 190

ANSWERS AND EXPLANATIONS:

Q1: B) 160

Explanation: The sales for Laptops in February is $160.

Q2: D) 58

Explanation: The sales for Cameras in April is $58.

Q3: B) 500

Explanation: Alice burns 500 calories while swimming.

Q4: B) 190

Explanation: Bob burns 190 calories while doing Yoga.

Q5: C) 45

Explanation: The average high temperature in NYC in March is 45°F.

Q6: D) 85

Explanation: The average high temperature in Miami in April is 85°F.

Q7: B) 62

Explanation: The temperature in Tokyo in April was 62°F.

Q8: D) Sydney

Explanation: Sydney had the highest temperature in January, which was 70°F.

Q9: B) 4

Explanation: The temperature difference between London and Paris in May was 64 - 60 = 4°F.

Q10: C) 32

Explanation: There are 32 Sophomores in the Science club.

Q11: D) 105

Explanation: The total number of students in the Drama club is 20 (Freshmen) + 22 (Sophomores) + 25 (Juniors) + 28 (Seniors) = 105.

Q12: A) Chess

Explanation: The Chess club has the least number of Seniors, which is 18.

Q13: C) 270

Explanation: The revenue for the Sales department in April was $270,000.

Q14: D) HR

Explanation: The HR department had the lowest revenue in February, which was $110,000.

Q15: B) 860

Explanation: The total revenue for all departments in March was 250 (Sales) + 170 (Marketing) + 320 (Engineering) + 120 (HR) = 860 ($1000s).

Q16: B) 200

Explanation: The revenue difference between Engineering and HR in May was 340 - 140 = 200 ($1000s).

Q17: A) 170

Explanation: The average revenue for the Marketing department from January to May is (150 + 160 + 170 + 180 + 190) / 5 = 170 ($1000s).

CHAPTER 16: SELF-DESCRIPTION INVENTORY

The Self-Description Inventory subtest is unlike any other section on the Air Force Officer Qualifying Test (AFOQT). While most of the test assesses your academic and technical skills, this subtest delves into your psychological makeup. It aims to understand your personality and behavior, which are crucial factors for a successful career in the U.S. Air Force.

Understanding the Self-Description Inventory Subtest

This subtest consists of a series of statements to which you'll respond, indicating how much you agree or disagree. These statements are designed to gauge various personality traits such as leadership, teamwork, stress management, and ethical behavior.

What to Expect

A series of statements related to behavior, feelings, and attitudes.

A Likert scale for each statement, usually ranging from "Strongly Agree" to "Strongly Disagree."

No time limit, but it's essential to be as honest and thoughtful as possible.

Strategies for Success

1. Be Honest

The primary rule for this subtest is honesty. Remember, there are no right or wrong answers here. Your responses should accurately reflect your feelings and attitudes.

2. Don't Overthink

It's easy to get caught up in analyzing what each question is trying to assess. While it's good to be thoughtful, overthinking can lead to answers that don't genuinely reflect your personality.

3. Understand the Context

While the test aims to understand you on a psychological level, remember that the context is your suitability for roles within the Air Force. Keep this in mind as you respond to the statements.

4. Consistency is Key

Be consistent in your responses. Contradictory answers can send mixed signals about your personality and behavior.

Sample Statements for Practice

To give you a feel for what to expect, here are some sample statements you might encounter in this subtest.

I thrive in high-pressure situations.

- Strongly Agree
- Agree
- Neutral
- Disagree
- Strongly Disagree

I find it difficult to trust people.

- Strongly Agree
- Agree
- Neutral
- Disagree
- Strongly Disagree

I am always punctual and value timeliness.

- Strongly Agree

- Agree
- Neutral
- Disagree
- Strongly Disagree

I prefer to follow rather than lead.

- Strongly Agree
- Agree
- Neutral
- Disagree
- Strongly Disagree

I am highly organized in both my personal and professional life.

- Strongly Agree
- Agree
- Neutral
- Disagree
- Strongly Disagree

I find it challenging to express my emotions.

- Strongly Agree
- Agree
- Neutral
- Disagree
- Strongly Disagree

I am open to receiving constructive criticism.

- Strongly Agree
- Agree
- Neutral
- Disagree

- Strongly Disagree

I often take risks without considering the consequences.

- Strongly Agree
- Agree
- Neutral
- Disagree
- Strongly Disagree

I value harmony and avoid conflicts in group settings.

- Strongly Agree
- Agree
- Neutral
- Disagree
- Strongly Disagree

These practice statements are designed to give you a comprehensive understanding of the types of questions you'll encounter in the Self-Description Inventory subtest. Take your time to consider each statement carefully and respond as honestly as possible. Remember, the goal is to provide an accurate portrayal of your personality and behavioral traits. By doing so, you're not only helping the Air Force assess your suitability for various roles but also gaining valuable insights into yourself.

NOTE: There are no right or wrong answers for these items.

CONCLUSION

This comprehensive guide has equipped you with the essential knowledge, strategies, and practice needed to excel in the Air Force Officer Qualifying Test (AFOQT). From breaking down the complexities of each subtest to offering invaluable tips from experienced Air Force officers, this book is your one-stop resource for AFOQT preparation.

But the journey doesn't end here. To further enhance your study experience, we're offering a free flashcards app that complements this guide. This interactive tool will help you review key concepts on-the-go and make your preparation more effective. Scan the QR code below to download the app and take your AFOQT preparation to the next level.

Made in United States
Troutdale, OR
12/23/2023

16391389R00144